Dedica

This book is dedicated, with love,

To my mother, who taught me good work ethics, values and the zest for life. She is also the *best* country cook!

To my father, who grew the delicious foods we ate and who is a daily example of kindness and goodness.

To my husband, Travis, who encourages me in every endeavor and has the patience to live with me!

And to Delia-Anne, our new, wonderful granddaughter.

Heart in Hand

Cooking with
Heart in Hand

Suzanne Winningham Worsham

Heart in Hand Inc., Clifton, Virginia, 1987

Library of Congress Catalogue Card No. 87-82558

ISBN: 0-9619445-0-1

Third Edition

Printed in the United States of America

Printed in the USA by

WIMMER
The Wimmer Companies, Inc.
Memphis • Dallas

Acknowledgments

To: The whole Heart in Hand staff, you help complete the total picture . . . it takes all of us to succeed.

To: Susan Achenbach, one of the nicest people I know. Also for her support, untireless work, and friendship. I couldn't have made it the first year in business without her.

To: Adora Payne for her help in keeping hearth and home organized. Our family truly loves you!

To: Mr. & Mrs. Raleigh E. Worsham for the use of their Key West, Florida home as a haven to finish the cookbook.

To: Mr. Grady Sparkman, for the hours locating Tennessee hams for me.

To: Mr. & Mrs. Elmer Winningham, my parents, for their love, support and "good bringing up."

To: Wanda Fitzpatrick, my sister, for her recipes.

To: Travis, my husband, for all his "tastings" through the years and all his support.

To: My daughters Ginny, Sherry, and Sarah. "Things" will get back to normal "a.c." (after cookbook).

To: Sara Stewart, my childhood mentor, thank you for taking such an interest in me and being the "swooshiest" person I know.

There are many people I would like to thank for their help and support in the creation of this cookbook.

To: Jann Aanestad for her execution of the cover design and related interior artwork and all the additional hours spent helping me.

To: Brenda Ference for her exquisite quilt drawings done on a tight schedule.

To: Diana Stagnato for the cover design and her friendship through the years.

To: Barbara Schmoyer for her hours of work editing and in helping the production of the cookbook. Many thank yous.

To: Ron Miller of Anytime Typesetting.

To: Juliet Verzolini for artistic support.

To: Susann Miller for her invaluable assistance in getting the book off the ground.

To: Shelva Rota for her many hours of typing, inspiration, and collaboration when it was really needed.

And last but not least, to all of our special friends—the fine people who have enjoyed dining at the Heart in Hand. Thank you!

Table of Contents

BRUNCH

LUNCH

DINNER

SUNDAY SOUTHERN SUPPERS

HOLIDAYS

SPECIAL OCCASIONS

Introduction

The menus and recipes I've gathered into this cookbook represent a lifetime of memories which I'm delighted to share with you. I hope the combinations of dishes provide you with meals which generate memories full of warmth and fellowship.

The Heart in Hand is a restaurant and catering business in Clifton, Virginia. This year we are celebrating our fifth year of operation. Owning and operating the Heart in Hand is a culmination of my lifelong love for cooking and entertaining. This cookbook captures the recipes and family traditions we share with our guests at the restaurant.

The following brief history of my family traditions and love for entertaining reveals the sources of my recipes and the memories associated with them.

I grew up in Cookeville, Tennessee, a small college town. My parents, Mr. and Mrs. Elmer Winningham (Geba and Daddy Shorty to the grandchildren) and I lived in a rural area, five miles from town. I was the third daughter, born two months early, as a real surprise on my mother's 36th birthday. I promptly demanded much attention since I weighed under three pounds and was in a small country hospital.

I've tried to remember back to my first impressions of being so interested in foods. I can recall the smells and textures of my father's newly planted gardens, the spring tilled soil, the first peas, lettuces and green onions of spring. He still plants a garden at age eighty and tenderly cares for it as he has his whole lifetime, planting our children's favorites for their annual summertime stay. I can remember the countless hours helping my mother canning and freezing the jams, jellies, pickles and relishes to see us through the seasons. I didn't realize then how much training I was receiving or what wonderful memories I would have from those times. We never had a meal that the produce wasn't the freshest, tastiest you could have. The table was always beautifully set with mothers dishes and creative center arrangement.

My mother instilled in me an independence to think for myself and accomplish any task set before me. Her discipline, "to do any job that's worth doing, right," was with me when I prepared my first dinner at age eight. I fried chicken, mashed potatoes, and cooked peas. It's probably still my favorite meal.

As I grew older I would exchange recipes with my sister Diane who lived in Detroit, Michigan. Her recipes were more ethnic than the country cooking we grew up eating. She and my mother bought me my first cookbooks which I poured over and usually prepared each recipe from the first to the last.

My school teachers at Capshaw Elementary School were aware of my interest and sometimes would send home recipes they had tried. I still have several recipes from Mrs. Henry, my second grade teacher. In High School when Home Economics was a required course, I was always frustrating my teachers because I wanted to "fancy up" our menus. In college I don't know if it was me or my family's great cooking that kept Travis, my husband, coming to our house day after day.

After we were married I decided to take on Julia Child's, Mastering the Art of French Cooking, Volume I and II. Every day for three months I cooked elaborate French meals exactly per her instructions. Finally one day Travis said, "Suzi, this food is wonderful, but can't we have a good old American hamburger?"

As the years passed by I took several cooking courses as well as doing quite a bit of entertaining. Travis played polo for several years in the Washington area and I usually was the person in charge of tailgate picnics and special buffets for visiting teams including a dinner for the British Polo Team.

One thing leads to another and I helped cater events for friends and business related functions while we were raising the three girls as well as running an antique and gift shop in Clifton.

Now, finally to how Heart in Hand Restaurant came about... While I was busy running the antique shop, Travis was busy building commercial buildings and restaurants in the Washington area. At one time, he was part owner of a restaurant in the Northern Virginia area. The little town of Clifton, where we lived at that time, was not condusive to business. Clifton is not near any major road or business center in Fairfax County and because of its size and remoteness had no drawing power to keep the few small shops going. We knew that to draw business, there had to be a drawing card—GOOD FOOD. Travis talked me into starting a small restaurant to entice ladies to come to lunch, shop, and stroll around in the historic little town. I thought he was crazy. One, I had no formal restaurant training, two, the town fathers were very anti-business, and three, everyone knows restaurants have the highest failure rate of any business.

Well, we opened. My first year I had as a partner Susan Achenbach. She took leave from her intensive care nursing duties for one year and we opened the doors October 29, 1982, with a deep commitment and much prayer on my part. From the first day of business we had customers and word of mouth made our business grow from one lunch room to serving six days and nights a week. We almost doubled our size as well as providing social and corporate catering in the Washington area.

I feel the charm of the restaurant is its decor, which is cozy, comfortable, stylish country. We use vivid blues, reds, and greens with many antique quilts as decor for the walls. Country flower arrangements and Southern antiques compliment each other. The display windows and mantels are always decorated in seasonal themes.

We picked the name Heart in Hand as a tribute to our forefathers who worked hard with their hands through the love in their hearts. I have a tin cookie cutter that is a two hundred year old replica of a heart in hand—thus our theme. We hope that each customer realizes how much hard work and love has made the Heart in Hand a special place.

I am delighted to say this is our fifth anniversary. The town is finally receptive to the joys of good business and the public relations, for the town, gained from it. We've had many famous people eat at our restaurant as well as you from next door. We have the philosophy that whether you're eating a two dollar cup of soup or paying for an extravagant catered affair, you're important. We've enjoyed having Nancy Reagan twice, William Casey, many theatre and movie people, including Academy Award winner William Hurt, who's first scene in one of his movies was filmed at our restaurant, plus, a special dinner for the French and American joint Chiefs-of-Staff. But our day to day business is the gracious customers we get locally and from afar, that have made the restaurant a success. There is never a day that I don't peek in the dining room from the kitchen when "goosebumps" appear, and I know you are eating Suzi Winningham Worsham's food. What a thrill!

Our whole family's lifestyle changed with the restaurant. Travis and I began working at the restaurant full time as well as our daughters, Suzanne Geneviere, Sherry Dianne, and Sarah Elizabeth. Susan Achenbach left to resume her nursing duties and we took over after that. We have since bought an old house to restore near the restaurant so we could be close to work as well as convenient for the children. Travis, in two years, has almost completed all the work and we're now hoping to expand our catering business.

Our hope is to continue serving good, well seasoned, prepared fresh daily foods, attractively presented. It's also our desire to serve you from our hearts through our hands, I hope true love comes through your cooking.

Enjoy,

Suzi

Quilt Collection

Foreword

As we proceed with our third printing I know many cooks are now counting calories, fat grams, etc. I have successfully substituted non-fat yogurt, mayonnaise, sour cream, low or no fat dressings in many of our recipes. The Herb Dip on page 188 is an excellent example of a recipe that can use substitutions.

Before you begin using our menus and recipes–always remember to use the freshest ingredients possible, fresh herbs and good quality spices. Your cooking will show the extra care!

The most simple or the most elaborate meal is enhanced by its table setting. Use your imagination to create unusual centerpieces; mix china patterns and silver, use vegetables and fruits combined with fresh or dried flowers for table arrangements. Use everyday objects in a new light. Don't take entertaining so seriously that you the host or hostess, can't enjoy your own food!

The smallest touches, a heart crouton, a mint sprig or a wedge of fruit can make a dish special...your family and guests will appreciate the extra touches.

And remember to taste, taste, taste as you cook!

Smokey Mountain Cabin

COUNTRY BREAKFAST

Skillet Eggs
Cornmeal Scrapple
Homemade Applesauce
Toast
Strawberry Preserves

Cornmeal Scrapple

This is a true, old recipe. The flavor is so wonderful it really is worth reviving!

Serves 10 to 12

2 cups ground pork	1 1/2 teaspoons rubbed sage
2 cups ground beef	dash of cayenne pepper
3 cups beef broth	1 cup cornmeal
2 teaspoons salt	hot vegetable oil
1/4 teaspoon pepper	

Combine pork, beef and broth in a medium saucepan, bring to a boil, stirring to crumble. Add seasonings. Gradually sprinkle in cornmeal, stirring constantly. Cook 30 minutes over low heat, stirring frequently.

Spoon into a greased 10-inch tube pan. Chill until firm. Cut into 1/2 inch slices, and fry in 1/2 inch hot oil until brown, turning once.

This makes a wonderful cold weather supper. Add mashed potatoes, cooked sauerkraut and a warm rice pudding.

Homemade Applesauce

Give your family or guests a real treat by preparing real applesauce. It is a little work with a big reward.

Makes 6 cups

6 pounds tart apples, peeled, cored and sliced	3/4 cups water
	1 1/2 teaspoons lemon juice
freshly grated nutmeg to taste	Sugar to taste

Place the apples, nutmeg and water in a heavy saucepan. Bring to a boil. Reduce heat and simmer uncovered for 30-35 minutes, stirring occasionally to prevent sticking or burning. This applesauce should be thick. Remove from heat, add lemon juice to prevent darkening, and add sugar for taste.

Skillet Eggs, see page 164.

Strawberry Preserves, see page 167.

BRUNCH A LA NEW ORLEANS

Mimosa Heart in Hand
Pain Perdu
Rum Baked Bananas
Special Oven Bacon
Pineapple Delight
Cajun Coffee

Mimosa Heart in Hand

Makes 1 (12-ounce) serving

1 jigger apricot brandy
1/2 goblet champagne
1/2 goblet freshly squeezed
   orange juice

fresh or canned apricot half
   for garnish

In a 12-ounce goblet fill half with orange juice, half champagne and jigger of brandy. Garnish with apricot half and sprig of mint.

Pain Perdu

This is the New Orleans version of French toast. Pain Perdu means lost bread or day old bread. A delightful use for leftovers!

5 eggs
1/2 cup granulated sugar
3 tablespoons brandy
2 tablespoons orange liqueur
1 teaspoon finely grated fresh
   lemon peel

1 teaspoon vanilla
8 (half-inch) thick slices of
   day-old French or Italian
   bread
vegetable oil
Powdered or cinnamon sugar

In a large, deep bowl, beat the eggs and granulated sugar with a wire whisk until they are frothy and well combined. Beat in the brandy, orange liqueur and lemon peel, then add the bread slices and turn them about in the egg mixture to moisten them evenly. Let the bread soak at room temperature for at least 30 minutes.

In a heavy 12-inch skillet, heat vegetable oil until it is very hot but not smoking. Fry the bread, three of four slices at a time, for 2 minutes on each side, turning the slices carefully with a wide metal spatula and regulating the heat so that they brown richly and evenly without burning. As they brown, transfer the bread slices to paper towels to drain.

Sprinkle the Pain Perdu with powdered or cinnamon sugar and serve at once. Serve with a pitcher of pure cane syrup or substitute 2 parts dark corn syrup to 1 part good molasses for the syrup.

Rum Baked Bananas

A hint of paradise

Serves 4

1/4 cup dark rum
1/4 cup dark brown sugar
3 tablespoons apricot jam
   or apricot preserves
2 tablespoons butter, melted
   and cooled

2 tablespoons strained fresh
   lemon juice
4 large ripe bananas, peeled
   and cut lengthwise into
   halves

Preheat oven to 350 degrees.

Combine the rum, brown sugar, apricot jam or preserves, melted butter and lemon juice in a small bowl and stir until the ingredients are well blended. Arrange the banana halves, cut side down and in one layer, in a shallow unbuttered baking dish large enough to hold them snugly. Spread the rum misture evenly over the bananas, then bake in the middle of the oven for 30 minutes, or until the bananas are tender. Serve at once.

Special Oven Bacon

This bacon is unusual, but a real taste treat.

Serves 4

1 pound bacon
3/4 cup brown sugar

1 heaping tablespoon flour
1/2 cup nuts, finely chopped

Lay bacon side by side on broiler pan with a bottom (to catch grease). Mix flour with brown sugar, sprinkle on top of bacon, then sprinkle nuts on top of flour mixture. Bake in 350 degree oven for 30 minutes. Remove immediately.

Cajun Coffee

Serves 8

4 cups strong black coffee
8 tablespoons molasses
1 cup heavy cream, whipped
   stiff

Freshly grated nutmeg
Dark rum (optional)

Mix coffee and molasses. Heat to very hot. Pour into 8 Irish whiskey mugs or coffee cups. Top with whipped cream. Dust with nutmeg. (Place 1 tablespoon of rum in each cup before adding hot coffee - stir.)

Pineapple Delight

A nice side dish
Serves 4

1 #2 can crushed pineapple, slightly drained
3 eggs, beaten
1/2 cup sugar

5 slices white bread, with crust, cut in cubes
1 stick butter (do not substitute)

Preheat oven to 350 degrees. Combine eggs, sugar and pineapple, add to bread cubes mixed in butter. Bake in covered casserole for 40 minutes.

BRUNCH WITH A SPANISH FLAVOR

Fresh Fruit Cup

Pineapple Dipping Sauce

Avocado Fan Calcutta

Victor's Spanish Omelet

Banana Muffins

Blueberry Muffins

Honey Butter Spread

Fresh Fruit Cup

Dice or section available fresh fruits. Be sure to use ripe, blemish free, attractive fruit. The combination is up to you. The pineapple dipping sauce is delicious with any assortment of fruit.

Pineapple Dipping Sauce

Makes 2 cups

1 cup heavy cream, whipped   1 tablespoon sour cream
2 tablespoons lemon gelatin
1/2 cup crushed pineapple
   with juice

Whip cream, add powdered gelatin, fold in crushed pineapple with juice and sour cream.

Avocado Fan Calcutta

The hot sauce has a hint of India in it!

Serves 4

2 tablespoons butter   1 tablespoon chili sauce
2 tablespoons vinegar   1 tablespoon Worcestershire
2 tablespoons sugar   2 avocados
1 tablespoon chutney

Heat sauce ingredients in top of double boiler until well blended and really hot.

To serve: On a large salad plate, put a pool of hot sauce. Arrange half an avocado in a fan shape on top of sauce. Garnish with watercress and lemon wedge.

Victor's Spanish Omelet

Victor has been on our staff for four of our five years in business. He is an outstanding omelet cook. His Spanish Omelet is the favorite on Sundays.

eggs	**butter**
Cheddar or montery jack cheese, grated	**Creole Sauce**

Break 2 or 3 eggs per person in small bowl. Beat with whisk until fluffy. Pour into buttered hot 8 or 9-inch non-stick coated omelet pan. Bring cooked eggs to center with fork as for scrambled eggs. Let sit just a few minutes. Add 1/4 to 1/2 cup grated cheese down middle of omelet, flip omelet into half moon shape. To serve; cover with a ladle full of Creole Sauce. Garnish with a dollop of sour cream and a sprinkling of chopped green onions.

Creole Sauce

Serves 6

1/2 cup green pepper, chopped	2 bay leaves
1/2 cup onion, chopped	sugar to taste
1/2 cup celery, chopped	Tabasco sauce to taste
2 cloves garlic, minced	salt to taste
3 tablespoons butter	pepper to taste
2 cups canned tomatoes	Worcestershire sauce to taste
1 can tomato sauce	1/2 teaspoon oregano
1 cup water	1/2 teaspoon thyme

Saute first 4 ingredients in butter, add tomatoes, tomato sauce, water, bay leaves and seasonings. Simmer 30 minutes. Remove bay leaf. Serve over omelet.

Banana Muffins

Makes 12 large muffins

1/2 cup butter, softened	1/8 teaspoon salt
1 cup sugar	1/2 cup raisins, chopped
2 eggs	1/2 cup pecans, chopped
2 cups flour	3 ripe bananas, mashed
1 teaspoon baking soda	1 teaspoon real vanilla

Preheat oven to 425 degrees. Combine butter and sugar. Add eggs, one at a time, beating well after each. Combine flour, soda and salt, add to creamed mixture. Fold in remaining ingredients. Pour into well-greased muffin pans. Bake for 20 minutes.

Miniature muffins can be made by using a miniature muffin pan, baking at 300 degrees for 15 minutes. Makes approximately 6 dozen. Great for large crowds or party. Can also be done with the Blueberry Muffins.

Blueberry Muffins

Everyone loves warm muffins out of the oven

1 egg	2 teaspoons baking powder
1/2 cup sugar	1/8 teaspoon salt
1/2 cup melted butter	3/4 cups milk
2 cups sifted flour	1 cup blueberries (well-floured)

Preheat oven to 425 degrees. Combine egg, sugar and shortening. Blend well. Sift dry ingredients together. Add to egg mixture. Add milk and blueberries. Mix *only* until flour is moistened. Pour into well-greased muffin pans. Bake for 20 minutes.

Honey Butter Spread

1/4 cup butter, softened	1/8 teaspoon ground
1/4 cup honey	cinnamon
	1/8 teaspoon ground nutmeg

Blend all ingredients thoroughly.

LOVIN' OVEN BRUNCH

Wanda's Brunch Casserole
Butter by the Gobs, Apricots
Martha's Bran Muffins
Orange Nut Muffins
Pear Honey

Wanda's Brunch Casserole

My sister Wanda Fitzpatrick, owns the Scarecrow Country Inn, a bed and breakfast establishment in Cookeville, Tennessee. She is an excellent cook and gave me this brunch recipe. It is a favorite of her breakfast guests.

Serves 10

1 pound bacon
14 hard boiled (shelled) eggs
1 large onion, finely chopped
2 tablespoons flour
2 1/2 cups milk

1 1/2 cups Cheddar cheese, grated
3 cups crushed potato chips
1 stick butter, melted

Preheat oven to 350 degrees. Fry bacon, reserve drippings. Slice hard boiled eggs lengthwise. Saute onion in bacon drippings, add flour. Stir, add milk, mix well and stir in cheddar cheese. In well-greased 11x13-inch pan layer eggs, pour cheese sauce over, crumble bacon on top, sprinkle with crushed potato chips. Drizzle melted butter over all. Bake for 1/2 hour.

Butter by the Gobs, Apricots

This dish was aptly named. It is a buttery treat as a side dish for any brunch.

Serves 12

2 28-ounce cans apricots, drained
1 pound light brown sugar

12 ounces Ritz crackers, finely crushed
2 sticks butter, (no substitute)

Preheat oven to 300 degrees. Grease 3-quart casserole. Layer apricot, brown sugar and crackers; cut butter into pieces and place on top. Bake for 1 hour.

Pear Honey

A wonderful kitchen gift.

About 3 pounds ripe pears (to make 9 cups chopped pears)
1 cup diced pineapple

1 lime, juice and grated rind
5 cups sugar

Wash, pare and core pears. Chop in food processor. Combine ingredients and bring to a boil. Cook slowly for about 20 minutes, stirring often. Pack in hot jars and seal according to manufacturer's instructions.

Martha's Bran Muffins

My childhood friend, Martha Marable Arnett, gave me this recipe. Now we're making it for our children, who are friends.

Makes 4 dozen 2" muffins

3 1/4 cups raisin bran
1 1/4 cups sugar
2 1/2 cups flour (unsifted)
3 teaspoons soda
1/2 tablespoon pumpkin pie
   spice

1 teaspoon salt
2 beaten eggs
1/2 cup oil
2 cups buttermilk
1/4 cup raisins
1/4 cup pecans, chopped

Preheat oven to 400 degrees. Combine first 6 ingredients in large bowl, mix in eggs, oil and buttermilk, add raisins and pecans.

Fill well greased muffin pans 2/3 full. Bake 15 - 20 minutes for regular muffin size and 15 minutes for small size.

Mix can keep in refrigerator for up to 6 weeks. Baked muffins keep well in refrigerator or can be frozen.

Orange Nut Muffins

An assortment of muffins always receives "aah"s. This is a good muffin for your repertoire.

Makes 12 muffins

2 cups all purpose flour
1 tablespoon plus 1 teaspoon
   baking powder
1/4 cup sugar
1 teaspoon salt

1 egg, beaten
1/2 cup orange juice
1/2 cup orange marmalade
2 tablespoons vegetable oil
1/2 cup chopped pecans

Preheat oven to 400 degrees. Combine dry ingredients; make a well in center of mixture. Add egg, orange juice, marmalade and oil, stir just until dry ingredients are moistened. Fold in pecans. Spoon batter into greased muffin pans, filling two-thirds full. Bake for 15 minutes.

This muffin is delicious served with **Gingered Cream Cheese**, see page 148.

Stars and Stripes

FIRST LADY NANCY REAGAN'S
HOLIDAY LUNCH WITH GEORGE WILL

We were honored to have Mrs. Reagan and Mr. Will visit our restaurant. Luncheon served to them that day was a mixture of light favorites and heartier holiday fare.

Nancy Reagan

Cream of Broccoli Soup
House Salad with Our Famous Citrus Dressing
Joannie's Crabmeat Quiche
Festive Cranberry Salad
Geba's Spoon Rolls
Coffee

George Will

Tennessee Ham Bone Soup
House Salad with Our Famous Citrus Dressing
Pan-Fried Catfish with Pecan Butter
Sauteed Fresh Vegetable Medley
Geba's Spoon Rolls
Coffee

We were honored to have First Lady Nancy Reagan as the guest of Mr. George Will, news columnist and TV panelist, twice at the Heart in Hand.

Her first visit was on December 23, 1985. It was a delightful time for her visit with all of our Christmas decorations around the restaurant, the fireplace going, and Christmas music in the air. My mother and father were up from Tennesee for the Christmas holidays and it was a real treat for them to meet Mrs. Reagan and Mr. Will. My mother told Mr. Will, "that she would know him in a blackberry patch anywhere"—translation—"you are famous!" Mrs. Reagan took our daughter Sarah's hand and strolled down the streets of Clifton.

Their second visit was a real surprise, August 7, 1987. An hour and one-half before their arrival we were made aware of their coming. What surprised looks on the faces of our other guests when they realized who was sitting next to them! I thanked Mrs. Reagan and Mr. Will for dining with us again and Mrs. Reagan said "It was her pleasure, our food is so delicious". We gave them both two Heart in Hand soup or coffee mugs as a small momento of their visit.

Cream of Broccoli Soup

Perfect creamy soup for winter and beautiful color for the holidays.

Serves 6 to 8

1 large bunch fresh broccoli
2 large onions
1/2 cup butter
1/2 cup flour
3 cups milk
2 cups heavy cream

1 tablespoon instant chicken
   granules (or really rich
   cooked down chicken broth)
1 teaspoon white pepper
salt to taste
half and half, for thinning

Wash broccoli, trim and peel tough ends and stems, cut into 2-inch chunks, slice onions. Cover broccoli and onions with water, boil until tender. Puree cooking broth and broccoli until smooth in food processor.

Make a roux in heavy stockpot or saucepan using butter and flour. Whisking constantly—add milk, heavy cream, chicken granules and pureed broccoli and onions. Heat carefully. Add salt and pepper. If needed, thin with half and half to desired consistency. Serve in individual bowls and garnish with a dollop of sour cream, a sprinkle of fresh dill, chopped, and heart pimento.

Winter House Salad

Use an assortment of greens for a healthy, attractive salad.

1 serving

Mixed Greens	Red Onion Rings
Orange and Grapefruit slices, peeled, seeded	Toasted Pecans
	Cherry Tomatoes
Julienne cooked Beets, drained	Our Famous Citrus Dressing

Our Famous Citrus Dressing

Makes 4 cups

2 lemons, remove seeds	1/2 cup sugar
1 orange, remove seeds	2 cloves of garlic
1/2 teaspoon salt	1 cup lemon juice
1 teaspoon, cracked black pepper	2 cups good olive oil or blended olive oil

Process finely lemons, orange, spices, sugar and garlic. Add lemon juices and oil. This thickens upon sitting. Mix thoroughly and thin with lemon juice or oil if necessary.

Joannie's Crabmeat Quiche

Joannie had the honor of cooking for Mrs. Reagan and Mr. Will. This is her delicious quiche recipe that was served that day.

Makes 1 (9-inch) pie

4 eggs	1 cup flaked crabmeat
1 1/2 cups heavy cream	1/4 cup green onions, chopped
1 tablespoon sour cream	
1/2 teaspoon pepper	1 tablespoon parsley, chopped
1/4 teaspoon Old Bay Seasonings	1 (9-inch) deep dish pie shell, unbaked
1/2 cup grated Cheddar cheese	

Preheat oven to 375 degrees. Combine eggs, creams and seasonings. Sprinkle other ingredients onto bottom of pie shell, pour cream mixture over. Bake for 35 minutes, or until well puffed and center set. Serve on individual plate with a dollop of sour cream, sliced green onion tops, and cherry tomato half.

Festive Cranberry Salad

A little something "extra" to dress up a plate.

2 apples
2 cups cranberries
2 whole oranges, seeded
3/4 cup sugar
1 cup pecans, chopped
1 3-ounce package orange
   flavored gelatin

1 3-ounce package raspberry
   flavored gelatin
1 14-ounce can crushed
   pineapple, drained, add
   juice to water
2 cups boiling water

Grind the apples, cranberries, and the oranges (including rind) in a food processor. Add the sugar, nuts and pineapple. Stir well.

Dissolve the gelatin in the boiling water and stir well. Add to the cranberry mixture.

Pour into a 9 x 13-inch pan and chill until set. Serve on lettuce leaves with a dollop of mayonnaise on each portion.

Tennessee Ham Bone Soup

Good, old-fashioned soup!

Serves 15 to 20

1 baked Tennessee ham bone
   (with some meat left on it)
3 quarts water
1 cup sliced carrots
1 cup sliced celery
1/2 cup chopped onion
1 10-ounce package frozen
   whole kernel corn
1 10-ounce package frozen
   lima beans

1 16-ounce can black-eyed
   peas, undrained
1 16-ounce can tomatoes,
   undrained
1 tablespoon sugar
1 tablespoon lemon juice
thyme to taste
hot pepper sauce
worchestershire
salt and pepper to taste

Break ham bone into 2 or 3 pieces. Place in large soup kettle. Add water; simmer 30 minutes. Remove bones, remove meat from bones. Chop meat and return to broth. Add carrot, celery and onion; simmer 30 minutes. Add remaining vegetables; simmer 1 to 2 1/2 hours. Add seasonings to taste.

Pan-Fried Catfish with Pecan Butter

People love our catfish! This is a great recipe.

Serves 6

6 8-ounce boneless farm raised catfish fillets	white cornmeal (preferably stone ground)
1 cup milk	Flour
2 eggs, beaten	Oil (light) for frying
3 teaspoons Seasoning Mix	Pecan Butter

Mix milk and egg, dip catfish in flour then in egg milk mixture then coat with seasoning mix added to cornmeal.

Fry in approximately 1/4 to 1/2 inch *hot* oil, turn only once and finish cooking in baking pan in 350 degree oven for 10 minutes. (Make sure oil is hot, catfish is completely coated with cornmeal mixture, and turn *only* once for beautiful crust and no oily taste.

Serve with lemon wedges and a dollop of Pecan Butter.

Seasoning Mix

1 teaspoon salt	2 3/4 teaspoon black pepper
1 teaspoon ground red pepper (cayenne)	1 1/2 teaspoon onion powder
1 tablespoon paprika	1 1/2 teaspoon oregano
2 3/4 teaspoon garlic powder	1 1/2 teaspoon thyme

Mix together. Use for seasoning on blackened fish, chicken, beef, seasoned toast. Great on anything!

Pecan Butter

16 tablespoons butter	1 teaspoon lemon juice
1/2 cup coarsely chopped toasted pecans	dash Tabasco or hot sauce

Whip all together in mixer or food processor. Keeps indefinitely.

Sauteed Fresh Vegetable Medley

Crisp, crunchy, and pretty!

Serves 6 to 8

1 cup carrots, julienned
1 cup turnips, julienned
1 cup squash, julienned
  (yellow or zucchini)
1/2 cup snow peas

3 tablespoon butter
  (no substitute)
salt and pepper
sugar

Julienne carrots, turnips, and squash into small strips. Steam in small amount of water until crisp and color sets (takes 3 to 5 minutes); drain. Add diagonally cut snow peas for color, butter, salt, pepper and a pinch of sugar, heat quickly. Shake pan to gild butter on all the vegetables.

Geba's Spoon Rolls, see page 126.

FIRST LADY NANCY REAGAN'S SUMMER LUNCH WITH GEORGE WILL

Nancy Reagan

Gazpacho
Mary's Curried Chicken Salad
Geba's Spoon Rolls
Coffee

George Will

Fresh Summer Vegetable Soup
Cheese Straws
Kentucky Hot Brown Sandwich
Geba's Spoon Rolls
Coffee

Gazpacho

All the flavors of summer in a bowl.

Serves 10

3 large green peppers
2 peeled cucumbers
1 red onion
3 ribs celery
4 large ripe tomatoes
3 cups tomato juice
1 cup olive oil
1 cup red wine vinegar

1 teaspoon garlic salt
1 teaspoon pepper
1 teaspoon dried basil
  (2 fresh)
1 teaspoon dried oregano
1/3 cup sugar
hot sauce to taste

Blend in food processor. Garnish with thin cucumber slice and heart shaped crouton.

Heart Crouton: Cut small hearts out of good quality bread, spread with butter or Herb Butter (see page 31), toast in oven until crisp.

Mary's Curried Chicken Salad

Mary cooked for Mrs. Reagan and Mr. Will on this day. She made a wonderful curried chicken salad as the special of the day and Mrs. Reagan chose that for lunch.

Serves 6

6 pound roasting chicken
1 cup celery, diced on
  diagonal
1 small crisp apple, diced
1 handful seedless grapes
1 3-ounce can crushed
  pineapple, drained
1/2 cup chopped, pitted dates
1/2 cup yellow raisins

1/2 cup green onions,
  chopped
1/2 cup chopped toasted
  almonds (save some for
  garnish)
1 1/2 cups mayonnaise
3 to 4 tablespoons heavy
  cream
Imported curry powder

Roast or boil chicken. Cool and dice the meat.

To mayonnaise, add cream and curry powder to taste. Combine with the chicken and fruit. Serve salad on a bed of greens, sprinkle almonds on top. Also serve copper penny sticks placed on plate around lettuce. (See page 76). Make carrot sticks instead of rounds in recipe.

Geba's Spoon Rolls, see page 126.

Fresh Summer Vegetable Soup

Growing up, we often canned or froze this recipe to use on cold winter days, but it tasted so special with the vegetables coming straight out of the garden.

Serves 6 to 8

4 pounds beef with the bone
6 peppercorns
1 onion, stuck with 3 or 4
  cloves (optional)
1/2 pound pork (country
  ham, fatty pieces or
  salt pork)
a few sprigs of parsley
celery stalks with a few of
  the leaves
1 cup butter beans

1 cup cut green beans
1 cup shredded cabbage
1 1/2 cups fresh corn
2 cups peeled, seeded, and
  finely chopped tomatoes
2 cups sliced okra
salt
thyme
Worcestershire
sugar
hot sauce

Brown meat well in a hot skillet. Place all of the beef into a large stockpot. Add the peppercorns and enough cold water to just cover the meat. Simmer for 5 to 6 hours. Halfway through the cooking, add onion, pork, parsley and celery. When the meat becomes tender, remove it from the pot. Strain the broth and return it to the pot. Heat to simmer. Add the vegetables and cook for 1 hour, simmering. Salt to taste. Remove all the fat from the soup; add seasonings and adjust.

Cheese Straws

Great for cocktails or soups, makes that "little something extra!"

Makes about 5 dozen

1 cup all-purpose flour, sifted
1/2 teaspoon baking powder
1 cup (4 ounces) shredded
  sharp Cheddar cheese

1/2 cup butter
3 tablespoons cold water

Preheat oven to 400 degrees. Combine flour and baking powder. Cut in cheese and butter with a pastry blender until mixture resembles coarse meal. Sprinkle water evenly over flour mixture; stir with a fork until ingredients are moistened.

Roll dough to 1/8 inch thickness on a lightly floured surface and cut into small hearts.

Place hearts on ungreased baking sheets. Bake for 12 minutes or until crisp. Place on wire racks to cool.

Note: This mixture can also be used in a cookie gun to make ridged stripes cut in squares. Also all the work can be done in a food processor.

Kentucky Hot Brown Sandwich

This dish was famous at the Brown Hotel in Louisville, Kentucky. This is a year-round favorite at the restaurant.

Serves 4

2 whole chicken breasts
  (3/4 pound each), cooked
4 1/2-inch thick slices white
  bread, trimmed
4 slices crisp bacon
1/2 stick butter
1/4 cup flour
2 cups milk, heated
1/4 cup grated Parmesan
  cheese

2 eggs, beaten
1 teaspoon salt
1/4 teaspoon pepper
nutmeg—freshly grated
  (to taste)
2 teaspoons lemon juice
1 cup shredded Cheddar
  cheese

Skin and bone chicken and slice each half lengthwise. Toast bread, butter lavishly and place in a 200-degree oven to crisp while preparing sauce. Melt butter and stir in flour and whisk until there are no lumps. Add hot milk and whisk until perfectly smooth. Cook, whisking constantly, until thickened. Add parmesan cheese. Stir about 1/2 cup of mixture into eggs, then pour this back into sauce and cook a minute longer, stirring all the time. Add salt, pepper, freshly grated nutmeg and lemon juice.

To assemble sandwiches: Place toast on a ovenproof platter and arrange chicken slices on top, allowing 1/2 breast per serving. Cover each with 1/2 cup of sauce and sprinkle each with 1/4 cup grated cheddar cheese. Place under broiler for about 1 minute or place in a 425-degree oven until speckled with brown. Arrange bacon crosswise on top and serve at once. Garnish with parsley and cherry tomatoes.

BRIDAL LUNCHEON

Colorful, elegant fare for a special occasion.

Kir Champagne Punch
Cucumber Bisque
Seafood Charleston
Oven Baked Rice
Sarah's Sour Cream Muffins
Fresh Strawberry Mousse
Maids of Honour

Kir Champagne Punch

A beautiful punch, light and festive.

Serves 16

1 (10-ounce) package frozen raspberries, partially thawed

1 (16-ounce) bottle club soda, chilled

1/2 cup creme de cassis, chilled

2 (750 milliliters) bottles champagne, chilled

Place one package raspberries in blender or food processor; puree until smooth. Pour raspberry puree into punch bowl with club soda and creme de cassis; stir gently to blend well. Slowly pour champagne down side of bowl. Stir gently.

A heart shaped ice ring or heart cubes are a nice addition as well as fresh mint garnish.

Cucumber Bisque

A refreshing, light soup.

Serves 6 to 8

6 medium to large cucumbers (peels removed)

2 medium yellow onions

2 teaspoons concentrated chicken base (or chicken granules)

1 cup hot water

4 cups Half and Half

6 tablespoons sour cream

1/2 teaspoon white pepper

1 1/2 teaspoons dried dill or 1 tablespoon fresh dill

Chop cucumbers and onions finely in food processor. Add chicken base dissolved in hot water, Half and Half, sour cream, pepper, dill. Mix well with wire whisk. Chill thoroughly. Serve with a fresh lemon twist and fresh dill sprig.

Seafood Charleston

This is a wonderful, creamy, rich dish. Elegant enough for dinner parties, too.

Serves 6

1 3/4 cups milk	2 teaspoons Worcestershire
3 tablespoons flour	2 egg yolks, well-beaten
1 stick butter (no substitute)	3/4 cup chopped
1/2 teaspoon salt	mushrooms, cooked
1/2 small onion, chopped	1/4 cup dry sherry
1 tablespoon green pepper	3/4 cup heavy cream
1 teaspoon paprika	3 pounds seafood: mixture of
1 tablespoon pimento,	shrimp, scallops and
chopped	crabmeat, cooked

Cook first 4 ingredients in large double boiler. When sauce thickens, add onion, green pepper, paprika, pimento and worcestershire sauce. Just before serving, add yolks, cream and dry sherry. Stir in mushrooms and seafood.

Oven Baked Rice, see page 31.

Sarah's Sour Cream Muffins, see page 63.

Fresh Strawberry Mousse

Serves 6

1 pint strawberries	1/4 cup sugar
2 (3-ounce) packages	1 pint whipping cream
strawberry flavor gelatin	

Crush the strawberries. Drain and reserve the juice. Add enough water to the juice to make 1 1/2 cups. Bring the juice to a boil and stir in gelatin. Dissolve and cool. Add strawberries and sugar. Whip cream until it stands in soft peaks and fold into strawberry mixture. Pour into individual parfait or wine glasses. Chill several hours or overnight. Garnish each with a dollop of whipped cream, strawberry and mint leaf.

Maids of Honour

Makes 5 1/2 dozen

1 1/2 cups butter, softened
1 cup sugar
3 egg yolks
3 cups all-purpose flour
1/4 teaspoon salt

1 1/2 teaspoons real vanilla
extract
1 cup strawberry jam
Filling

Preheat oven to 350 degrees. Cream butter; gradually add sugar, beating until light and fluffy. Add egg yolks, one at a time, mixing well after each addition. Add flour, salt, and vanilla, mixing well.

Shape dough into 1-inch balls; press dough into greased 1 3/4 -inch muffin pans to form shells. Spoon 1/2 teaspoon jam into each shell. Spoon filling over jam to fill shells.

Bake for 20 minutes. Remove from pans while warm. Cool.

Filling

2 eggs
3/4 cup sugar
3 tablespoons dry sherry
1 teaspoon grated lemon rind
3/4 cup finely ground
almonds

1 tablespoon all-purpose
flour
1/4 teaspoon salt
1/4 teaspoon ground nutmeg
1/4 teaspoon ground
cinnamon.

Beat eggs until light and frothy; gradually add sugar, beating well. Stir in sherry and lemon rind.

Combine almonds, flour, salt and spices, mixing well. Stir into egg mixture, blending thoroughly.

DOMINION VALLEY GARDEN CLUB LUNCHEON

Old Fashioned Cream of Tomato Soup
Heart Cheese Straws
Chicken Suzanne with Herb Butter
Oven Baked Rice
Glazed Steamed Asparagus
Geba's Spoon Rolls
Heart in Hand Raspberry Ice Cream
Easy Ice Cream Cookie

Old Fashioned Cream of Tomato Soup

Joannie makes wonderful soups. This is her recipe and is one of our best soups. Sarah devours cups of it when she stops by the restaurant after school.

Serves 10

1 stick butter
1/2 cup flour
4 cups milk
2 1/2 pounds canned diced
   tomatoes
1 1/2 cups tomato juice

1 1/2 cups prepared bloody
   mary mix
2 1/2 teaspoons salt
2 teaspoons pepper
1/2 cup sugar
2 cups heavy cream

Make a roux in large pot using butter and flour, careful, not to brown. Add remaining ingredients, simmer 15 minutes. Garnish each serving with a dollop of sour cream and green chopped onions.

Heart Cheese Straws, see page 23.

Chicken Suzanne

Our absolutely number one favorite dish at the restaurant. We have had more requests for this recipe than any other.

Serves 6

6 boneless (8-ounce) chicken
   breast halves
1 cup flour
1 egg beaten with 1 cup milk

3 cups good quality fresh
   bread crumbs
1/2 to 1 cup light cooking oil.

Dip chicken breasts in flour, dip in egg/milk mixture, then thoroughly coat in bread crumbs.

Saute in hot oil until well browned on each side. Cook until done (do not overcook).

Serve with a dollop of herb butter.

Herb Butter

1/2 cup chopped green onions
1/2 cup chopped fresh parsley
2 cloves garlic
1 teaspoon basil
  (2 tablespoons fresh)
1/2 teaspoon oregano
  (1/2 tablespoon fresh)
1 teaspoon marjoram
  (1 tablespoon fresh)

1 teaspoon tarragon
  (1 tablespoon fresh)
1 teaspoon dillweed
  (1 teaspoon fresh)
1 teaspoon black pepper
Dash of tabasco
1 pound unsalted butter

Mix all above thoroughly in food processor.

The herb butter is delicious on French bread toasted, or toast triangles. Can also be used on steaks, hamburgers, veal scallopini or steamed vegetables.

Oven Baked Rice

Always cooks beautifully and holds well in a warm oven too!

Serves 6

1/2 cup butter
1 1/2 cups rice, uncooked
1 medium onion, chopped
1/2 cup mushrooms
1/4 cup slivered almonds

1/4 cup chopped celery
1 teaspoon parsley flakes
2 cans beef bouillon or 2 cans
  chicken stock

Preheat oven to 350 degrees. Saute rice, onion, mushrooms, almonds, and celery in butter until rice begins to brown. Add parsley and 2 cans of broth. Bake in covered baking dish for 45 minutes or until all liquid is absorbed.

Glazed Steamed Asparagus

Asparagus is always delightful and can make a meal special.

Serves 6

24 stalks fresh asparagus　　　**1 teaspoon sugar**
4 tablespoons butter

　　Cut off thick ends of asparagus. Peel stalk from the bottom up to the tips. leave tips intact. Place in large frying pan, add boiling water to cover. Cook until crisp-tender, 3 to 5 minutes for small spears, 5 to 8 minutes for large spears, drain. DO NOT OVERCOOK. Melt butter over asparagus, sprinkle sugar and shake until each spear is gilded with butter and sugar.

Geba's Spoon Rolls, see page 126.

Heart in Hand Raspberry Ice Cream

Sometimes the easiest to make is the best!

Makes 1 to 1 1/2 quarts.

2 boxes 10-ounce frozen　　　**1/8 cup creme de cassis**
　raspberries　　　　　　　　　**2 1/2 cups whipping cream**

　　Mix in ice cream maker according to your machine directions. For individual servings, garnish with a cherry and mint leaf.

Easy Ice Cream Cookie, see page 82.

ROCKY RUN GARDEN CLUB LUNCHEON

House Salad-Viniagrette
Raspberry Chicken
Fresh Broccoli Almondine
Glazed Baby Carrots
Geba's Spoon Rolls
Mocha Mousse Parfait
Heart in Hand Butter Tea Cookies

Summer House Salad

Per serving

Mixed greens
Cucumber, peeled, scored,
    and sliced

Green pepper circles
Red onion circles
Carrot, grated

Attractively arrange vegetables on mixed greens.

Viniagrette Dressing, see page 95.

Raspberry Chicken

This is an elegant, different luncheon dish. The ladies groups love it. (Men do, too!)
Serves 12

4 tablespoons butter
1 medium onion, minced
1/2 cup diced canned tomatoes
1/4 cup raspberry vinegar
    (or tarragon vinegar)
2 tablespoons creme de cassis
1 1/2 cups heavy cream

2 10 ounce boxes frozen red
    raspberries, thawed
salt and pepper to taste
6 whole chicken breasts,
    divided to make 12 servings
flour
1/2 cup clarified butter or oil

In a large frying pan, saute chicken breasts which have been lightly dredged in flour, in butter or oil, until light brown. Cover and cook 12 to 15 minutes until chicken breasts are cooked through, check to make sure when pricked with a fork that the juices run clear. DO NOT OVERCOOK.

Saute the onion in 4 tablespoons butter until melted. Add rest of ingredients. Boil down until desired consistency and flavors have mingled. Adjust seasonings (a little lemon juice can be added just before serving). The taste should be a sweet-tart flavor.

Fresh Broccoli Almondine

Serves 8

3 pounds fresh broccoli
2 tablespoons toasted, sliced
    almonds

melted butter

Wash broccoli, cook in salted water until crisp-tender. Drain, drizzle butter over and scatter nuts on top.

Glazed Baby Carrots

The baby carrots in the market are perfect for this.

Serves 8

32 young carrots or	1/2 teaspoon salt
5 cups (3-inch) carrot sticks	1/2 cup melted butter
1 1/2 cups water	2 teaspoons sugar

Cook carrots in water with 1/2 teaspoon salt added, just until tender. Drain well. Heat butter and sugar, add carrots, cook on high heat until glaze forms around carrots.

Mocha Mousse Parfait

Rich, creamy, and can be made ahead.

Serves 6

6 ounces semisweet chocolate bits	1/2 cup whipping cream
	2 tablespoons powdered sugar
2 teaspoons hot water	4 eggs, separated
1 teaspoon coffee powder	2 teaspoons coffee liqueur

Combine chocolate bits and water in small saucepan, cook over low heat until melted, add coffee powder. (Can be microwaved).
Place melted chocolate, cream, sugar, and egg yolks in blender container. Cover; blend at medium speed for 3 minutes, stiffly beat egg whites. Fold in egg whites and coffee liqueur.
Pour into 6 small parfait glasses or demitasse cups. Refrigerate for 2 hours or until set. To serve, put a dollop of whipped cream on each and serve with a Heart in Hand Butter Tea Cookie.

Geba's Spoon Rolls, see page 126.

Heart in Hand Butter Tea Cookies, see page 129.

BUSINESSMAN'S LUNCH

Bull and Bear Martini
Mary's Rich Onion Soup
Marinated Flank Steak Salad
Herb Butter Toast
Brownie a la Ginger with Caramel Sauce

Bull and Bear Martini

Serves 1

1 3/4 ounces dry gin	green olive, garnish
1/4 ounce dry vermouth	pickled onion, garnish

Frost 3-ounce cocktail glasses. Fill Martini pitcher with cracked (not crushed) ice. Ice should be dry and hard frozen. Measure out the exact ingredients for the number of drinks required, pouring in the dry gin first (gin should "smoke" as it settles over the cold ice), then the dry vermouth. Stir briskly until drink is very cold. Strain at once into frosty, stemmed cocktail glasses. For martinis "on the rocks," use prechilled Old-Fashioned glasses and pour the liquor over cubes of ice.

Garnish with colossal green olive and large pickled onion on drink pick.

Mary's Rich Onion Soup

All our cooks have good tastebuds. Mary is no exception!

Serves 12

1/2 pound butter	1 tablespoon salt, to taste
2 large onions, sliced	6 cups beef consomme
1 cup flour	6 cups water
large pinch of sugar	1/2 cup red wine
1 tablespoon pepper	

Melt butter, add onions and pinch of sugar. Cook slowly for 30 minutes; add flour and cook for a few more minutes until lightly browned. Add remaining ingredients, simmer covered, 45 minutes. Adjust seasoning if needed.

Marinated Flank Steak Salad

Makes a beautiful large salad, so good in hot summertime!

Serves 4

2 pounds flank steak
1/2 cup red wine vinegar
1 cup oil
1 cup tomato juice
1 tablespoon garlic
1 tablespoon crushed
  rosemary

dash hot sauce
1 teaspoon pepper
1/2 teaspoon salt
2 tablespoons chopped fresh
  basil

Marinate steak in above ingredients 8 hours or overnight. Broil or cook on grill 3 1/2 minutes on each side until rare to medium. Thinly cut on diagonal across grain.

Serve on a platter by making a salad with a bed of lettuce, layering the steak slices, red sweet onions, tomatoes, monteray jack cheese (cut in strips) and artichoke hearts. Serve with vinaigrette. Garnish with fresh basil.

Herb Butter Toast, see page 31.

Brownie a la Ginger with Caramel Sauce

Really Good Brownies, see page 196.
Very Good Vanilla Ice Cream, see page 56.

Caramel Sauce:
Makes 1 1/2 cups

2 tablespoons butter
1 1/3 cups brown sugar
1/2 cup water
1 teaspoon real vanilla
1/4 teaspoon salt

1/2 cup strong coffee
1/2 cup heavy cream
finely chopped fresh ginger to
  taste or chopped preserved
  ginger

Cook first three ingredients until the liquid coats back of spoon. Cool, add remaining ingredients, heat for a few minutes. To serve: pour on top of brownie with a scoop of ice cream.

Be careful when reheating, turns grainy.

LIGHT LUNCH FOR LADIES

Wonderful Frozen Fruit Salad
Tea Sandwiches
Pimento Sandwich
Benedictine Sandwich
Country Ham Butter
Banana Bread - Gingered Cream Cheese
Coffee Kahlua Ice Cream
Aunt Lula's Mud Hen Cookies

Wonderful Frozen Fruit Salad

Serves 10 to 12

1 can apricots, chopped
(1 pound)
1 can pears, chopped
(1 pound)
1 bottle red cherry halves
(maraschino)

1 can crushed pineapple
(1 pound)
1 can mandarin oranges
(11 ounce can)
2 bananas, sliced
1 cup pecans, chopped

Drain fruits, set aside, prepare dressing.

2 eggs, beaten
4 tablespoons vinegar
4 tablespoons sugar
1 small jar marshmallow
cream

1 (8-ounce) carton heavy
cream, whipped

Combine eggs, vinegar and sugar in heavy pan. Cook until thick, stirring constantly. Remove from heat. Cool. Add marshmallow cream and whipped cream. Add fruit and mix well. Pour into individual molds. Freeze for 24 hours. Garnish with a dollop of whipped cream and a fresh strawberry.

Pimento Sandwich, see page 147.

Benedictine Sandwich

Another Kentucky recipe.

Makes about 1 1/2 cups

2 medium-sized cucumbers,
peeled and seeded
1/2 medium-sized onion,
peeled
1 large (8-ounce) package
cream cheese, softened

homemade mayonnaise
salt
cayenne pepper
green vegetable coloring

Grate cucumbers and drain well. Grate onion. Blend these into cream cheese and add enough mayonnaise to make a soft spread. Season lightly and add drops of coloring to make a delicate green. Do not use a blender as it makes mixture runny.

To make sandwiches: Remove crusts from thinly sliced bread. Spread a slice generously with Benedictine and cover with another slice to make a rather thick sandwich. Cut in halves or triangles.

Country Ham Butter

Chop cooked country ham in food processor, add equal amount of butter. Puree until smooth, put on bread triangles or biscuits.

Autumn Pumpkin Bread - Gingered Cream Cheese, see page 148.

Coffee Kahlua Ice Cream, see page 142.

Aunt Lula's Mud Hen Cookies

My Great Aunt Lula Looper from Albany, Kentucky was a wonderful cook. I enjoyed visiting my cousin, Susie Qualls, her granddaughter, and eating at Great Aunt Lula's. We always thought these cookies had the funniest name. But they are GOOD!.

Makes 24 2-inch squares

1/2 cup butter	1 teaspoon vanilla
1 cup sugar	1/2 teaspoon salt
3 eggs (reserve 2 egg whites)	1 cup nuts, chopped
1 1/2 cups flour	1 cup brown sugar
1 teaspoon baking powder	

Preheat oven to 350 degrees. Mix first 7 ingredients together. Spread very thin in a greased 9 x 13-inch pan. Sprinkle with chopped nuts.

Beat egg whites stiff and add brown sugar. Spread over nuts and bake for 30 minutes. Cut into squares while hot.

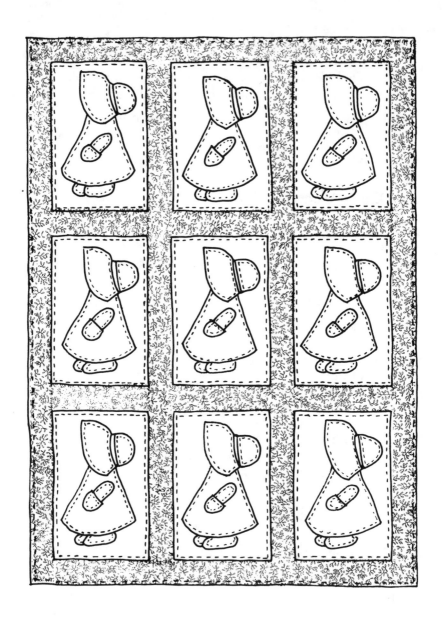

Sunbonnet Sue

SUMMER LUNCHEON

Warm from the Oven Corn Sticks

Chilled Potato Onion Soup
Tarragon Seafood Salad
Buttermilk Cake
Raspberry Sauce

Warm from the Oven Corn Sticks

Makes 14 Cornsticks

1 1/2 cups cornmeal
  (stoneground)
1/4 cup all-purpose flour
2 teaspoons baking powder
1/4 teaspoon baking soda

1 teaspoon salt
1 cup buttermilk
2 eggs, beaten
2 tablespoons shortening,
  melted

Preheat oven to 400 degrees. Combine cornmeal, flour, baking powder, soda, and salt; mix well. Add buttermilk and eggs, stirring just until dry ingredients are moistened. Stir shortening into batter.

Heat well-greased cast-iron corn stick pans in a 400-degree oven for 3 minutes or until very hot. Spoon batter into pans, filling two-thirds full. Bake for 25 minutes or until lightly browned.

Chilled Potato Onion Soup

Exquisite!

Serves 12

6 potatoes
2 large onions, sliced
1 stick butter
1/2 cup flour
3 cups milk
2 cups heavy cream

1 tablespoon chicken bouillon
  granules
1 teaspoon white pepper
salt to taste
Half and Half, for thinning

Peel and quarter potatoes. Cover potatoes and onion slices with water, boil until tender. Cool. Puree potatoes, onions and cooking broth in food processor.

Make a roux in heavy stockpot using butter and flour. Whisking constantly, add milk, heavy cream, chicken granules and pureed potatoes. Heat carefully. Add pepper and salt to taste. If needed, thin with Half and Half to desired consistency. Serve in individual bowls with a dollop of sour cream and chopped green onion tops.

Soup can be served hot and garnished with cooked crumbled bacon or with grated cheddar cheese.

Tarragon Seafood Salad

Sophisticated dish...Very good!

Serves 4 main courses, 6 appetizer courses

4 to 6 ripe medium to large
  tomatoes
1 1/2 pounds medium shrimp,
  shelled and deveined
  (reserve 6)
1 pound lobster meat (picked
  through)
1/2 cup tiny peas, fresh
  or frozen
1/2 cup finely chopped diced
  pimento

4 green onions cut into 1/2"
  diagonal pieces
salt and freshly ground black
  pepper to taste
1 cup or more Tarragon
  Dressing
Watercress
4 or more fresh fruits per
  plate for garnish (melon,
  grapes, strawberries,
  pineapple)

Boil 4 quarts water, drop in shrimp, bring back to boil, drain immediately, cool...add to lobster.

Prepare dressing.

Mix dressing with other ingredients. Hollow tomatoes to make a serving container, scallop or petal edges, turn upside down and drain. Fill tomatoes with seafood salad. Arrange on plates with watercress and fresh fruits.

Tarragon Dressing

1 egg (room temperature)
2 egg yolks
1/3 cup dijon mustard
1/4 cup tarragon vinegar
1 teaspoon dried tarragon or
  1 tablespoon fresh tarragon

pinch sugar
1 cup best quality olive oil
1/2 to 1 cup light oil

Mix all ingredients except oils in food processor. Slowly add oil to make a mayonnaise dressing.

Buttermilk Cake

My cousin, Mabel Whittaker, makes wonderful desserts. She would often let me "help" her bake when I would visit as a child.

Makes 1 10-inch cake

1 cup shortening (solid)	1 teaspoon orange extract
2 cups sugar	1 teaspoon lemon extract
1 cup buttermilk	2 cups sifted all-purpose
1 teaspoon soda	flour
4 eggs	1/2 teaspoon salt

Preheat oven to 350 degrees. Add soda to buttermilk, cream shortening, gradually add sugar, beating well. Add eggs, one at a time, beating well after each addition. Combine flour and salt; add to creamed mixture alternately with milk, beginning and ending with flour mixture. Mix well after each addition. Stir in flavorings.

Pour batter into a well-greased floured 10-inch tube pan. Bake for 45 to 60 minutes. Cool in pan 10 to 15 minutes; remove from pan, and cool completely.

To serve, put a pool of raspberry sauce on dessert plate. Cut cake into fingers and add a dollop of whipped cream.

Raspberry Sauce

1 10-ounce carton frozen raspberries (thawed)	1 tablespoon good orange liqueur

Puree in food processor. Chill.

REHEARSAL DINNER

Shrimp Cocktail with Best Cocktail Sauce
Filet Mignon with Roquefort Butter
Baked Potato
Tomato stuffed with Spinach Souffle
Crusty French Bread
Classic Pecan Pie
Geba's Iron Skillet Chocolate Pie

Shrimp Cocktail

Classic and always a hit

Serves 1

6 large shelled, cooked and deveined shrimp, chilled	lettuce lemon wedge

Best Cocktail Sauce, see page 132.

Place 6 large chilled shrimp in lettuce lined sherbet glass with Best Cocktail Sauce in middle, garnish with lemon wedge.

Filet Mignon with Roquefort Butter

A special dish for a special occasion.

Serves 4

4 (8 to 10 ounces each), 3-inch thick beef tenderloin	3 tablespoons butter

Saute the beef in butter in very hot pan until brown. Cook 3 to 5 minutes on each side for medium-rare on grill or hot skillet. Serve with big dollop of Roquefort Butter.

Roquefort Butter

1/2 cup butter	dash worcestershire
1/2 ounce roquefort cheese	dash hot sauce
1 tablespoon brandy	

Mash all above ingredients together, serve at room temperature.

Baked Potato

Scrub Idaho baking potato thoroughly. Prick several times with a fork. Spray with vegetable cooking spray (or rub with vegetable oil). Bake in hot oven. Split an x on top, squeeze to puff potato. Serve immediately with butter, sour cream, freshly grated pepper or chopped chives.

Tomato Stuffed with Spinach Souffle

Serves 6

Preheat oven to 350 degrees. Scoop pulp from medium tomatoes. Fill with Spinach Souffle mixture. Sprinkle with bread crumbs and parmesan. Bake for 20 minutes.

Can be made ahead. Cook before serving.

Spinach Souffle

This is good anytime.

Serves 6

1 10-ounce package frozen
  chopped spinach
1 small onion, chopped
1 tablespoon vinegar
1 (3-ounce) package cream
  cheese

1 teaspoon salt
1/4 teaspoon pepper
1/4 teaspoon nutmeg
2 eggs

Cook spinach according to package directions, adding onion and vinegar to saucepan, drain well. Place all ingredients in blender or food processor, process until well blended.

Classic Pecan Pie, see page 178.

Geba's Iron Skillet Chocolate Pie, see page 178.

NEW ORLEANS STYLE DINNER

Crabmeat Stuffed Mushrooms
Blackened Grouper
Baked Oven Rice
Baked Eggplant Creole
Crusty French Bread
Sweet Potato Pie
Cajun Coffee

Crabmeat Stuffed Mushrooms

This is our number one appetizer sold at the restaurant.

Serves 12

48 mushrooms
1 pound cream cheese
1 1/2 cups lump crabmeat
2/3 cup parmesan, grated
2 tablespoons Old Bay
  seasoning
1 tablespoon garlic powder

1 tablespoon onion powder
1 teaspoon white pepper
1 tablespoon hot sauce
1 tablespoon Worcestershire
1 tablespoon lemon juice

Preheat oven to 325 degrees. Remove stems from mushrooms. Wash caps well; drain on absorbent toweling. Process all remaining ingredients in food processor just enough to be a lumpy mixture (do not overprocess). Stuff mushrooms with crab mixture. Bake 10 to 15 minutes – Run under broiler to brown. To serve, arrange on platter with parsley and cherry tomatoes.

Blackened Grouper

With Cajun Fever sweeping America, our blackened grouper has been a huge success.

Heat a cast iron skillet SMOKING HOT. Dip 8 to 10-ounce grouper fillets in melted butter, roll in Victor's Blackening Mixture, blacken on each side in skillet. Continue cooking until fish flakes easily. DO NOT OVERCOOK. Can be blackened then put in 375 degree oven for approximately 15 minutes to finish cooking.

Victor's Blackening Mixture

Makes 1 cup.

4 tablespoons Old Bay
  seasoning
2 tablespoons garlic powder
1 tablespoon thyme
1 tablespoon oregano
1 tablespoon paprika

cayenne pepper to taste
1 tablespoon onion powder
1 teaspoon white pepper
1 tablespoon garlic salt
1 tablespoon salt

Mix above ingredients. Store in tightly sealed container.

Baked Oven Rice, see page 31.

Baked Eggplant Creole

Eggplant is a favorite down in New Orleans.

Serves 4 - 5

1 medium eggplant, peeled
  and diced
3 tablespoons butter
3 tablespoons flour
3 large tomatoes, chopped
1 onion, chopped

1 green pepper, chopped
1 tablespoon sugar
1/2 bay leaf, crumbled finely
1/4 teaspoon ground cloves
1 teaspoon salt
bread crumbs, for topping

Preheat oven to 350 degrees. Peel and dice eggplant, put in saucepan, cover with water and boil for 10 minutes, drain.

Melt butter, blend in flour, add remaining ingredients and cook 5 minutes. Put eggplant in a casserole or oven proof container; pour vegetable mixture over top. Cover with bread crumbs and dot with butter. Bake for 30 minutes.

Sweet Potato Pie

Terribly Southern and Terribly Good!

Makes 1 9-inch pie.

2 cups cooked sweet potatoes,
  mashed
4 eggs
1 cups brown sugar
juice of one orange
juice of 1/2 lemon

1 cup heavy cream
1/2 cup butter
cinnamon, to taste
nutmeg, to taste
allspice, to taste
9-inch unbaked pie shell.

Preheat oven to 350 degrees. Add butter to hot mashed sweet potatoes and mix until blended. Add cream, sugar, fruit juices and egg yolks. Mix thoroughly and flavor with spices to taste.

Beat egg whites until stiff enough to stand in peaks and fold into potato mixture. Pour into pastry shell and bake for 30 to 40 minutes or until firm in center. Serve with whipped cream flavored with sherry, sprinkle with toasted chopped nuts.

Any winter squash can be substituted for the cooked sweet potatoes.

Cajun Coffee, see page 5.

SPRING DINNER

Spring Chicken with Rice Soup
Poached Salmon Steak, Mousseline
Glazed Asparagus
Steamed New Potatoes
Sarah's Sour Cream Muffins
Deep Dish Rhubarb Pie
Very Good Vanilla Ice Cream

Spring Chicken with Rice Soup

A light, vegetable soup, just right for the cool evenings of Spring.

Serves 12

1 (6-pound) hen	1 large onion, chopped
16 cups water	1/2 tablespoons salt
2 stalks celery	1 teaspoon pepper
1 onion	2 carrots, cut into diagonal
1 carrot	slices
2 stalks celery, cut into	1/2 teaspoon sage
diagonal slices	3/4 cup raw rice

Combine first 5 ingredients in large stockpot and simmer 1 1/2 to 2 hours. Cool.

Remove chicken and strain broth.

To the strained broth add chicken; shredded, and rest of ingredients. Simmer until vegetables and rice are done.

A few julienned snow peas added just before serving adds color and crunch to the soup.

Poached Salmon Steak

A beautiful, thick salmon steak is delicious, nutritious and easy to prepare.

Serves 6

1 lemon	1 teaspoon peppercorns
2 tablespoons tarragon	1/2 bay leaf
vinegar	3/4 cup carrot, sliced
2 onions, sliced	6 sprigs parsley
2 stalks celery, chopped	6 salmon steaks, 1/2 pound
1 teaspoon salt	each

Cut lemon into 4 large slices. Place all of the ingredients, except the salmon, in the bottom of a poaching pan. Arrange the salmon on top of the vegetables and add enough water to barely cover the fish. Slowly bring to a gentle boil, then reduce the heat and simmer until the fish flakes easily. Be careful not to overcook. Carefully remove the fish with a perforated spatula to a heated platter. Serve immediately.

Mousseline Sauce

Makes 1 cup

To make mousseline sauce add 1 cup heavy cream whipped to the following hollandaise.

Hollandaise

1 cup sweet butter, softened
4 egg yolks
3 teaspoons lemon juice
pinch salt

few drops Tabasco
1 cup heavy whipping cream,
  whipped

Divide soft butter into 3 parts. In the top of a double boiler over hot (not boiling) water, put the egg yolks and 1 part of the butter. Stir constantly with a whisk until the butter is incorporated. Add each portion of the butter in the same manner. Do not let the water come to a boil at any time. Remove saucepan from the heat and beat for 2 minutes with a whisk. Add the lemon juice and seasoning. Replace over the hot water and beat 2 minutes longer. If it curdles, immediately beat in 1 to 2 tablespoons of boiling water.

Food Processor Hollandaise:

1/2 cup sweet butter, melted
4 egg yolks
2 tablespoons lemon juice

pinch of salt
few drops tabasco

Process egg yolks and seasonings about 30 seconds. With machine running slowly add the hot butter in a steady stream until the sauce is thickened.

Glazed Asparagus, see page 32.

Steamed New Potatoes

Tiny new potatoes are always a sign that spring is here.

Serves 6 - 8

18 small new red potatoes,
  washed
butter

salt
pepper
parsley

Peel a small strip around the middle of each potato. Put in saucepan with just enough water to cover. Bring to a boil, cook until done, about 30 minutes. Drain, put butter on top, roll each potato around in butter. Salt, pepper and sprinkle chopped parsley on top.

Deep Dish Rhubarb Pie

This is my sister Wanda's recipe. We all think it is the best rhubarb pie. If you've never tried rhubarb, try this.

1 recipe double pie crust
  (see page 155)
4 cups rhubarb, chopped
3 cups sugar

4 heaping tablespoons flour
4 eggs separated
1 stick butter, cut up

Preheat oven to 350 degrees. Line a deep dish 2-quart casserole with pastry; layer rhubarb, sugar and sprinkle flour over top. Beat egg yolks and pour over first layer, add cut up butter. Beat egg whites till light and frothy, pour over all. Put vents in top pie crust pastry and cover pie. Bake for 45 minutes.

Rhubarb is available year round, fresh in springtime and chopped frozen in the freezer sections of your supermarket.

Very Good Vanilla Ice Cream

Hilda Ayres, a very good family friend from Knoxville, Tennessee, gave me this recipe. She says, "It's always very good!" The original recipe called for the ingredients to be cooked but they work wonderfully uncooked.

Makes 1/2 gallon

4 egg yolks
1 1/8 cups sugar
pinch salt
1 quart whole milk

1/2 pint whipping cream,
  whipped stiff
1 teaspoon vanilla

Blend egg yolks, pinch of salt, and sugar in food processor. Add some of the milk to make a smooth mix. Pour into bowl, add rest of milk and vanilla; fold in whipped cream. Freeze in ice cream maker according to machine directions.

Sarah's Sour Cream Muffins, see page 63.

SUNDAY SOUTHERN SUPPERS

Our Sunday Southern Suppers were introduced at the Heart in Hand to bring back the old fashioned feeling of Sundays long passed. Times when families spent many hours preparing and enjoying good, down-home food. We *love* preparing the old, traditional recipes and hope that you will too!

VIRGINIA SMOTHERED CHICKEN DINNER

Virginia Smothered Chicken
"Don't Stir the Pot" Green Beans
Real Mashed Potatoes
Geba's Famous Biscuits
Deep Dish Rhubarb Pie

Virginia Smothered Chicken

A comforting dish quickly made and delicious.

Serves 4

1 3-pound chicken, cut into 8 pieces	1/4 teaspoon thyme
1/2 cup butter	1 cup boiling water
1/2 cup carrots, chopped fine	1 teaspoon fresh tarragon
1 onion, chopped fine	Salt and pepper
	All purpose flour

In a large, heavy skillet melt butter and heat to foaming stage. (DO NOT BROWN). Add onions, turn down heat. While onions are cooking, lightly dust chicken with flour. Raise heat, then brown chicken in butter with onions. Add carrots, water, and thyme, cover with a tight fitting lid. Cook on lowest heat possible for 1 1/2 hours. Leave lid on and shake pan occasionally to prevent sticking. DO NOT PEEK. Add tarragon, salt and pepper fifteen minutes before serving. DO NOT USE DRIED TARRAGON.

"Don't Stir the Pot" Green Beans

These are true Southern beans and are delicious with a slice of fresh red onion or relish.

Serves 10

1/2 pound salt-cured bacon or hog jowl	2 teaspoons salt
4 cups water	1 tablespoon sugar
3 full quarts fresh green beans, snipped into 1 1/2-inch pieces	Ground red pepper to taste

Put pork and water in heavy dutch oven. Simmer 30 minutes. Add beans, sugar, and red pepper. Cover and bring to boil, reduce heat and cook slowly for 1 1/2 to 3 hours. Remove lid and boil liquid down if too much in pot. "DO NOT STIR THE BEANS" Mother always said because they just don't come out the same.

Real Mashed Potatoes

6 servings

5 medium-sized Idaho
  potatoes
1 teaspoon salt
1/2 cup butter, cut into 8
  pieces

Ground white pepper to taste
(optional)

Wash and pare the potatoes and cut into quarters. Place in saucepan and cover with hot water. Add salt. Bring to boil and cook on high heat 20 minutes or until done.

Drain and mash with potato masher. Add butter, pepper, and more salt to taste. Fluff with masher and serve piping hot!

Geba's Famous Biscuits

My mother, Geneva Winningham, "Geba" to the grandchildren, makes "melt in your mouth" tiny biscuits. Customers of her antiques business, friends, and family from all over the world expect these flaky, delicious morsels whenever they visit and no one has been disappointed yet!

Makes 36 bite-size biscuits

3 cups self-rising flour
3/4 cup lard or shortening

1 full cup buttermilk

Preheat the oven to 475 degrees. Put flour in bowl, add shortening in small pieces. Work with fingers until mixture resembles coarse corn meal. Make a well in center of dry mixture. Add buttermilk, work in with fingers. Do not overwork dough. Turn dough out onto lightly floured pastry board and "turn over or knead" quickly. Roll out 1/2-inch thick and cut with 1-inch cutter. Place on greased baking sheet with sides of biscuits touching each other. Bake 8 to 10 minutes until lightly brown and serve immediately.

Use the grease that country ham has been fried in to grease the pan. You can also take a spoon and lightly brush the tops of the biscuits with the ham flavored grease. I've also used melted clarified butter to do the job.

Dip biscuit cutter into flour to keep the dough from sticking.

Deep Dish Rhubarb Pie, see page 56.

Fox Chase

SALISBURY STEAK DINNER

Salisbury Steak
Sour Cream Scalloped Potatoes
Buttered Green Beans
Sunshine Salad
Sarah's Sour Cream Muffins
Banana Meringue Pudding

Salisbury Steak

When Travis and I were in college, Mildred Netherton, a neighbor, occasionally used to help mother cook. She made delicious salisbury steak, yeast rolls and breads. Somehow Travis always knew when to show up at our house for dinner.

Serves 6

2 to 3 pounds ground round
salt
pepper

Shape ground round into 6 large flat patties. Gild a large iron skillet with oil and brown the beef patties. Salt and pepper to taste. Remove patties. To the accumulated fat in pan add 1 heaping tablespoon *flour* and brown, add 3 cups tomato juice, 2 tablespoons vinegar, 1/2 teaspoon ground cloves, 1 teaspoon sugar, 1 teaspoon salt, and 1 cup finely chopped onions. Allow to come to a boil, return meat patties, cover, and simmer for 30 to 40 minutes.

Sour Cream Scalloped Potatoes

This is mother's recipe. A good dish for family dinners or company.

Serves 6

4 cups sliced cooked potatoes
1/2 cup onion, finely chopped
2 tablespoons butter
1 cup sour cream
2 tablespoons water

2 eggs well beaten
1 teaspoon salt
white pepper to taste
1 cup shredded Cheddar
  cheese

Preheat oven to 350 degrees. Cook potatoes in salted water until done DO NOT OVERCOOK. Saute onion with butter, combine with sour cream, water eggs, salt and pepper. Place potatoes in buttered 1 quart casserole. Pour sauce over potatoes. Top with grated cheese and bake for 20 to 25 minutes.

Buttered Green Beans

Buy tender, crisp green beans as a change from country beans.

Serves 6

2 pounds green beans,   1 teaspoon sugar
  ends removed   2 tablespoons butter
2 teaspoons salt

Fill a large saucepan with water. Bring to a boil Drop green beans in and cook 10 minutes. Drain. Melt butter in pot, add beans, then add salt, pepper, and sugar. Shake pan to coat each bean with butter. Cover and let sit or serve immediately.

Sunshine Salad

9 servings

1 3-ounce package lemon   3/4 cups sugar
  flavored jello   1 cup whipping cream,
1 cup boiling water   whipped
1 8 1/4 oz. can crushed   1 cup shredded Cheddar
  pineapple, undrained   cheese

Dissolve gelatin and sugar in water. Add pineapple, cool. Fold in whipped cream and cheese. Spoon into lightly oiled 9-inch square pan; chill until firm. Cut into squares. Garnish with a dollop of mayonnaise, grated yellow cheese, on bed of curly lettuce.

Sarah's Sour Cream Muffins

At the age of 5, Sarah would stand on upside down milk crates to make rolls at the restaurant. She still enjoys making them. This is a good recipe for children and also easy for a busy cook.

Makes 12 muffins

2 cups self-rising flour   1 1/2 stick butter, melted
1 cup sour cream

Preheat oven to 350 degrees. Lightly combine above ingredients and put into greased muffin pan. Bake for 20 minutes.

Banana Merinque Pudding

There is nothing more homey or really comforting than this rich dessert.

Serves 8

1/3 cup flour
3/4 cup sugar, divided
dash of salt
2 cups milk
1 tablespoon butter

3 eggs, separated
1 teasoon real vanilla
1 11-ounce box vanilla wafers
6 ripe bananas

Preheat oven to 425 degrees. In a heavy saucepan, stir flour and 1/2 cup of sugar, add salt. Whisk in enough milk to form paste, then add remaining milk. Cook over moderate heat until it thickens. Add butter and cook a few minutes more. Slowly add some of the hot mixture to the beaten egg yolks. Pour into saucepan with rest of hot mixture. Cook over low heat until mixture coats your spoon. DO NOT COOK TOO HOT OR LONG as egg yolks will curdle. Stir in vanilla.

Alternate one third of vanilla wafers, one third sliced bananas in a 2 quart casserole. Cover with one third of custard mixture. Repeat layers twice.

Beat egg whites stiff with mixer. Add remaining 1/4 cup sugar. Beat until glossy. Spread over pudding. Bake in hot oven for 5 minutes or until golden brown. Serve warm or cold.

MUSTARD GLAZED HAM STEAK DINNER

Mustard Glazed Ham Steak
Real Mashed Potatoes
or
Baked Oven Rice
Spring Peas in Cream Sauce
Quick Light Rolls or Bread
Pineapple and Carrot Salad
Apple Dumplings with Sauce

Mustard Glazed Ham Steak

This is so good! Easy too!

Serves 6

1 1 1/2 - 2 inch thick center cut ham steak (already cooked ham)	Dry mustard Brown sugar Milk

Preheat oven to 275 - 300 degrees. Place ham steak in oven-proof pan a little larger than ham steak. Mix one part mustard to two parts brown sugar to make a dry paste; enough to cover top of ham slice. Pour milk into pan almost to top of ham slice. Bake in slow oven until tender and milk thickens around ham (approximately 45 minutes).

Real Mashed Potatoes, see page 59.

Baked Oven Rice, see page 31.

Spring Peas in Cream Sauce

The first green peas of Spring are such a treat, especially in a rich cream sauce.

Serves 6

3 cups shelled green peas	1/2 tablespoon flour
1 tablespoon sugar	1 tablespoon butter
NO SALT	1 cup heavy cream

Bring 4 cups water to a boil in a 4 quart saucepan. Add peas slowly to keep water boiling. Add sugar. Boil rapidly until done (10 to 25 minutes). DO NOT OVERCOOK . Drain. In same saucepan melt butter, stir in flour, cook for 2 minutes, whisk in heavy cream, cook until thickened. Add peas, serve.

The new Sugar Snap peas in pods, sliced on the diagonal, cooked 3 to 5 minutes, are also delicious in the cream sauce.

Quick Light Rolls or Bread

The aroma of these rolls fills the house with "old-timey" smells, with not much work.

Makes 12 rolls or 1 loaf

2 tablespoons vegetable
   shortening
1 cup water, boiling
1/4 cup sugar
1/2 teaspoon salt
1/4 cup lukewarm water

1 teaspoon sugar
1 package (2 1/2 teaspoons)
   active dry yeast
4 cups flour
1 egg

Preheat oven to 425 degrees. Mix first 4 ingredients. Cool to lukewarm. Dissolve yeast in 1/4 cup lukewarm water and the 1 teaspoon sugar. Combine yeast mixture with first mixture, add egg and 2 cups flour, beat well, adding remaining flour, stir until moistened. DO NOT KNEAD. Let rise until double in bulk, about 1 hour. Make into 12 rolls or 1 (9x5-inch) loaf. Grease a 9-inch square pan, place rolls side by side nearly touching or place loaf in greased pan. If desired, brush tops with melted butter. Cover with tea towel and let rise in warm, draft free spot for 1 hour. Bake 15 - 20 minutes for rolls or 30 - 35 minutes for loaf.

Pineapple and Carrot Salad

Pretty as a picture, good too!

Serves 8

1 package lemon jello
1 cup hot water
1 cup pineapple juice
1 cup crushed pineapple

1 cup carrots, grated
1/2 teaspoon salt
1 cup raisins
   (golden if available)

Drain can of crushed pineapple and reserve 1 cup juice. Dissolve jello in 1 cup hot water, add salt and pineapple juice. When jello starts to thicken, add grated carrots, 1 cup drained pineapple and raisins. Pour into a mold.

For easy release of salad, spray mold with vegetable cooking spray.

For individual servings place on a leaf of lettuce, with a dollop of mayonnaise and green sliced olives.

Apple Dumplings

My father loves these dumplings. There is nothing more "old-fashioned" than apples cooked this way.

Serves 6

6 large apples pared
    and sliced
1/2 cup sugar
1 cup water
1/8 teaspoon freshly grated
    nutmeg
1/8 teaspoon cinnamon

2 tablespoons butter
2 cups flour
2 teaspoons baking powder
1 teaspoon salt
2/3 cup shortening
1/2 cup milk

Preheat oven to 375 degrees. Sift together flour, baking powder, and salt; cut in shortening. Add milk and stir until moistened. Roll 1/4-inch thick on lightly floured surface. Cut into 6-inch squares.

Place apple slices in center of each square. Sprinkle each apple generously with sugar, cinnamon, and fresh nutmeg; dot with butter. Fold corners to center and pinch edges together, turn pinched edges under. Place 1-inch apart in a greased baking pan. Boil 1/2 cup sugar with water to make a thin syrup. Spoon the syrup over dumplings; sprinkle with sugar. Bake for 35 minutes. Serve hot with sauce.

If you dare, rich vanilla ice cream on side is delicious.

Sauce

I like thin sugar sauce.

1 cup sugar
1 cup water

freshly grated nutmeg
    (to taste)

Boil to desired thickness.

BEEF POT ROAST
AND VEGETABLES DINNER

Beef Pot Roast and Vegetables
Beet Salad
Quick Light Rolls or Bread
Clifton Cherry Cobbler

Beef Pot Roast and Vegetables

This dish was a favorite to cook on Sundays. We put it into the oven before Sunday School and church, and it was ready when we got home. The house always smelled so good when we walked through the door.

Serves 6

3-pound beef chuck roast
all purpose flour
vegetable oil
salt and pepper
1 pound carrots, peeled and
  cut into 3-inch sticks
6 medium potatoes, peeled
  and quartered

6 small onions, peeled
2 1/2 cups boiling water
1 tablespoon Worcestershire
1 teaspoon Kitchen Bouquet
2 cloves garlic
1 bay leaf

Preheat the oven to 350 degrees. Dredge the roast in flour, shake off excess. Brown the meat on all sides, in a little oil, in a heavy Dutch oven. Season with salt and pepper. Add the vegetables and all other ingredients. Cover, place in oven. Bake approximately 2 hours.

Remove meat and vegetables and place on an attractive platter. Pass the gravy which was made automatically in the pot, around the table separately. (If gravy needs to be thickened, boil down a few minutes and taste for seasoning.) Serve with a good horseradish or mustard.

Beet Salad

Serves 8

2 envelopes unflavored gelatin
1/2 cup cold water
1 1/2 cups beet juice
1 cup cider vinegar
1 heaping tablespoon
  horseradish

1 tablespoon lemon juice
1/2 cup sugar
1 teaspoon salt
2 cups shredded cooked beets
2 cups shredded cabbage

Soften gelatin in cold water. Heat beet juice. Add to gelatin, stir to dissolve. Add other liquid ingredients. Chill until syrupy. Fold in shredded vegetables. Pour into 1 1/2-quart mold which has been sprayed with vegetable cooking spray. Chill until firm.

Quick Light Rolls or Bread, see page 67.

Clifton Cherry Cobbler

As a child in Tennessee, Mrs. Bice, my next door neighbor, would let me climb her sour cherry trees and pick for pies. Mother would make fresh cobblers and package the remaining cherries in the freezer. When fall and winter rolled around, I would "sneak" the sugared frozen cherries a few at a time out of each container, thinking they wouldn't be missed. I thought WRONG!

Today, I have a wonderful sour cherry tree in my yard which produces enough cherries for real Clifton Cherry Cobbler to serve at the restaurant.

Serves 12

1 cup butter (no substitute)
2 cups self-rising flour
2 cups milk
1 1/2 cups sugar (see note)
4 to 6 cups red sour cherries
    (fresh or frozen)

1/2 teaspoon almond extract
1/4 to 1/2 cup sugar
1/4 cup butter
1/4 cup sliced almonds

Preheat oven to 350 degrees. Put butter in ovenproof roaster size pan (11"x16 1/2") and melt in oven. Whisk flour, sugar (1 1/2 cups), milk, and almond extract to make a batter. Remove pan from oven, add batter, sprinkle cherries on top. Scatter extra sugar (1/4 to 1/2 cup), dots of butter, and almonds on top. Return to oven and bake until batter is golden brown and puffed around the fruit. Takes 30 to 40 minutes. Delicious with homemade vanilla ice cream.

This recipe can be halved.

This is a basic recipe to make apple, peach, blueberry or blackberry cobblers.

Apple, use 4 cups homemade applesauce or 4 to 6 cups sliced apples. cinnamon and nutmeg for flavoring, pecans on top.

Peach, use 4 to 6 cups peeled sliced peaches (fresh or frozen). Add almond flavoring and nutmeg. Almonds on top.

Blueberry, use 4 to 6 cups berries with mace as flavoring. Sprinkle brown sugar on top.

Blackberry, use 4 to 6 cups berries, add extra sugar on top if berries are real tart.

If a more moist cobbler is desired, add 1 cup liquid to each fruit, i.e. orange juice, water, or with 2 or 3 tablespoons liqueur mixed into batter. Creme de Cassis for blueberry or blackberry. Peach or apricot brandy for peaches. Applejack for apples or Kirsch in cherries.

Cherry Basket

CHICKEN AND DUMPLINGS DINNER

Chicken and Dumplings
Cooked Cranberry Mold
Pickled Okra
Copper Pennies
Rummed Raisin Pie

Chicken and Dumplings

There is nothing more old-fashioned or satisfying than a steaming bowl of chicken and dumplings. Any age appreciates this dish.

Serves 8

1 stewing hen, about 5 to 6 pounds	1 onion
10 cups water	2 celery stalks
3 teaspoons salt (or to taste)	2 carrots
6 peppercorns	2 bay leaves

Dumplings

1/4 teaspoon white pepper	4 tablespoons shortening
2 cups flour, self-rising	fresh parsley, chopped
1/2 cup ice water	

In a large stockpot put chicken, water, salt, peppercorns, onion, celery, carrots and bay leaves. Bring to a boil. Lower the heat and simmer, covered; until the chicken is tender, about 1 1/2 to 2 hours.

Skim the fat from the broth. Remove the chicken, discard the skin and bones and cut chicken into bite-size pieces; also remove cooked vegetables, cut into small pieces and return chicken and vegetables to broth. Let cool to room temperature. May be done ahead.

In a bowl combine white pepper, flour and shortening; blend with finger tips. Add ice water and mix well. Spoon dough into a well floured surface and roll it out 1/4 inch thick. Cut into 1-inch x 2-inch rectangles. Shake off excess flour.

Bring the broth to a slow boil, add the dumplings and cook until tender, about 5 minutes. Serve in deep soup bowls with a sprinkling of freshly chopped parsley.

Cooked Cranberry Mold

Nutritious as well as delicious

Serves 8

2 cups cranberries
1 cup water
1 cup sugar
1 1/2 tablespoons unflavored gelatin

2 tablespoons water
1/2 cup celery, chopped
1/2 cup red apple, chopped
1/2 cup pecans, chopped

Cook cranberries in 1 cup water until tender. Do not overcook. Add sugar, cook 5 more minutes. Dissolve gelatin in 2 tablespoons water, add to cranberries.

Cool until syrupy. Add celery, apple, and nuts. Put in 1 quart decorative mold or 8 inch square pan which has been sprayed with vegetable cooking spray.

Pickled Okra

Makes about 4 pints

2 pounds tender okra, about 3 inches long and cut with as much stem as possible
4 small hot red-pepper pods or 1/8 teaspoon crushed dried hot red pepper for each jar
4 1/2 inch slices of fresh ginger

4 cloves garlic, peeled
3 cups white vinegar
2 cups water
1/3 cup pure granulated salt
1 tablespoon celery or mustard seed (optional)

Wash okra well, then drain. Prick okra with fork and pack lengthwise with points alternately down and up into hot sterilized pint jars. Put 1 pepper pod, 1 garlic clove, and 1 ginger slice in each jar. Combine vinegar with water, salt and celery seed in saucepan and bring to boil. Pour at once over okra, filling to within 1/2 inch of top. Seal at once. Then process in boiling-water bath for 5 minutes. Let okra stand several weeks before serving to allow flavor to develop. Serve as appetizer or as meat accompaniment.

Copper Pennies

This is a great, colorful relish. Everyone loves it!

Serves 8 to 10

2 pounds (5 cups) carrots,
   sliced
1 medium sweet onion, cut in
   round slices
1 small green pepper, sliced
1 can tomato soup
1/2 cup light salad oil

3/4 cup sugar
3/4 cup vinegar
1 teaspoon prepared mustard
1 teaspoon Worcestershire
1 tablespoon salt
1 teaspoon pepper

Cook carrots until they are tender, but DO NOT OVERCOOK. Cool and drain. Add onion and green pepper slices. Mix other ingredients and pour over vegetables. Cover and refrigerate at least 24 hours. Serve either hot or cold. Keeps indefinitely.

Rummed Raisin Pie

This pie is the perfect ending for a delightful nostalgic meal!

Serves 6

1/4 cup dark rum
1 cup seedless raisins
2 1/4 cups milk
3/4 cup brown sugar
4 tablespooons cornstarch

2 eggs, separated
1 tablespoon butter
1 teaspoon real vanilla
4 tablespoons sugar
1 (9 inch) baked pastry shell

Preheat oven to 300 degrees.

Soak raisins in rum overnight. Scald 2 cups milk in top of double boiler. Mix sugar with cornstarch, moisten with 1/4 cup milk, add egg yolks and blend thoroughly. Pour into hot milk and cook, stirring constantly until thick and smooth. Add raisins and butter and beat well. Remove from heat, add vanilla and stir to blend. Pour into baked pastry shell.

Beat egg whites until foamy. Gradually add 4 tablespoons sugar, beat until stiff peaks form. Spread on cooled custard in pieshell. Bake about 30 minutes until meringue is browned.

WINTER AND SUMMER PORK RIB DINNERS

WINTER

Wonderful Winter Pork Ribs
Sweet and Sour Sauerkraut
Mashed Potato Cakes
Skillet Fried Onions
Quick Light Rolls or Bread
Shelva's Rice Pudding

SUMMER

Sensational Summer Pork Ribs
Summer Barbeque Sauce
Scalloped Summer Squash
Fresh Greens Wilted Salad
"Can of Corn" Jalapeno Corn Bread
Georgia Peach Ice Cream
Easy Ice Cream Cookies

Wonderful Winter Pork Ribs

Pork Ribs are hearty and flavorful. A perfect dish for a cold day.

6 servings

5 pounds meaty pork ribs   salt and pepper
1 teaspoon red pepper flakes

Preheat the oven to 400 degrees. Place the ribs in a large saucepan and add enough water to cover them. Add the red pepper flakes and about 1 teaspoon salt. Bring to a boil. Simmer for 1 hour or until tender.

Remove the ribs from the pot and place them meaty side up in a large baking pan. Season with salt and pepper. Bake until browned, about 20 minutes.

Sweet and Sour Sauerkraut

2 tablespoons bacon drippings   freshly ground pepper,
  or shortening   to taste
1 large onion, finely chopped   1 bay leaf, crumbled
2 large apples, pared, cored   4 pounds drained fresh
  and thinly sliced   sauerkraut (usually in dairy
1/2 cup red wine   or meat case)
2 tablespoons sugar   4 cups beef broth or water
1 teaspoon salt   1 tablespoon vinegar

Heat bacon drippings in a large, heavy saucepan. Add the onion and saute for a few minutes or until soft. Add apple slices and cook a few minutes longer. Stir in wine, broth, vinegar, sugar, salt, pepper and bay leaf and bring to boiling. Remove from heat . Add sauerkraut. Cover tightly and cook over very low heat for about 30 minutes, stirring now and then. Just before serving, boil down until the mixture thickens.

Mashed Potato Cakes

We always made these cakes on a flat, black iron griddle. Children love these.

Serves 6

4 medium sized potatoes   1 egg
  salt, black pepper to taste   4 tablespoons flour
1 small onion, finely chopped

Boil the potatoes with jackets on, peel and mash. Add salt, pepper, egg and flour. Refrigerate to cool. Form into balls. Return to refrigerator. Flatten balls and saute until brown on both sides in skillet with melted butter. Serve on a platter around sauerkraut, barbecued spareribs, roast pork, etc., with fried onions on top of each potato cake.

Skillet Fried Onions

Old fashioned, and nothing smells better than onions frying in the kitchen.

Serves 6

5 cups thinly sliced onions
1/2 cup bacon drippings or
  vegetable oil
2 teaspoons sugar

salt
freshly ground black pepper
  to taste

Peel the onions and cut in slices about 1/2 inch thick. Do not soak in water. Place onions in a heavy 12-inch skillet containing the hot melted fat; then salt, pepper, and sugar. Have the heat high at first, as the onions begin to brown, lower the heat and let them simmer until done, stirring them occasionally to prevent burning or sticking. When onions are brown and soft they are done. Season to taste.

Quick Light Rolls or Bread, see page 67.

Shelva's Creamy Rice Pudding

My good friend and near-by neighbor, Shelva Rota, is an excellent cook as well as flower arranger. She has assisted me many times ar catered events. Her family loves this old-fashioned recipe, and so will you!

Serves 6

3 cups scalded milk
1 tablespoon butter
1 1/4 cups cooked rice
1/2 cup sugar

1/4 teaspoon salt
1/2 cup raisins
2 eggs, slightly beaten

Preheat oven to 325 degrees. Mix milk and next 5 ingredients. Slowly stir into the eggs. Turn into a greased 1 1/2 quart casserole. Set in a pan half-full of hot water. Bake for about 1 hour, stirring 1 or 2 times during first 30 minutes.

Sensational Summer Pork Ribs

Succulent and spicy, perfect for a lazy summer day and backyard barbeque.

Yield: 12 regular servings or 6 rib lovers servings

6 pounds spareribs (well trimmed)	**Summer Barbeque Sauce**

Cut spareribs into serving size pieces (about 3 to 4 ribs per person). Place ribs, bone side down, on grill over slow coals. Grill 1 1/2 hours, turning frequently. Brush ribs with Summer Barbeque Sauce, and cook 10 to 15 additional minutes on each side. DO NOT COOK TOO FAST. Watch carefully the last 15 minutes.

Summer Barbeque Sauce

Yield: about 1 quart

2 cups water	**1 onion minced**
1 1/4 cup catsup	**1 1/2 teaspoons red pepper,**
1/3 cup Worcestershire	**ground**
1 tablespoon paprika	**3/4 teaspoon pepper, freshly**
1 teaspoon dry mustard	**ground**
4 cloves garlic	

Combine all ingredients in a large saucepan, mixing well. Bring to a boil; reduce heat to medium. Cook, uncovered, 30 minutes, stirring occasionally.

Scalloped Summer Squash

Try to find local, homegrown squash. You'll notice the flavor difference.

Serves 8

8 medium summer squash	**1 cup milk**
1 large onion	**2 tablespoons melted butter**
2 eggs lighly beaten	**1 cup fresh bread crumbs**
1/2 teaspoon pepper	**2 cups grated sharp cheddar**
1 teaspoon salt	**cheese**

Preheat oven to 350 degrees. Cut squash in 2-inch cubes. Cook with sliced onions for 10 minutes; drain. Arrange in greased casserole. In mixing bowl, combine eggs, pepper, milk, butter, salt and 1 cup of cheese. Pour over squash. Sprinkle remaining cheese on top. Bake for 30 minutes.

Fresh Greens Wilted Salad

Early Spring greens, spinach, leaf lettuces, even good old iceberg take to this treatment.

Serves 6 to 8

6 slices bacon
bacon drippings
1/2 cup sliced green onion
1/4 cup vinegar (apple cider)
1/4 cup water
1 teaspoon sugar

1/2 teaspoon salt
black pepper (freshly ground)
  to taste
8 cups greens (torn)
6 radishes, thinly sliced
1 hard cooked chopped egg

Cook bacon until crisp; drain, reserving pan drippings. Crumble bacon, and set aside.

Combine greens, onions, and radishes in a salad bowl. Sprinkle with crumbled bacon, and set aside.

Add vinegar, water, sugar, salt and freshly ground pepper to drippings in pan; bring to a boil. Pour warm dressing over greens and toss lightly to coat well. Sprinkle hard cooked chopped egg on top of salad.

"Can of Corn" Jalapeno Corn Bread

Many times I'll ask Joannie, at the restaurant, to do a task and she invariably answers "can of corn". This recipe is for a New Jersey girl who really took to Southern cooking.

Serves 9

1 cup yellow corn meal
1 cup cream style corn
1 cup grated Cheddar cheese
1/2 cup vegetable oil
1/2 cup buttermilk
1 teaspoon baking soda
1/2 teaspoon salt

2 eggs, beaten
2 Jalapeno peppers, chopped
  fine
2 tablespoons bacon drippings
3 tablespoons pimentos,
  chopped

Preheat the oven to 400 degrees. Mix all ingredients (except for bacon drippings) in bowl. Put bacon drippings in a 9" x 9" pan or black skillet. Heat in oven until drippings cover bottom of pan. Pour batter into pan and bake for 20 to 25 minutes.

Georgia Peach Ice Cream

The essence of summer. Ripe, rich, creamy ice cream...the best!

Yield, 2 quarts

3 eggs
3/4 cups sugar
1/4 cup firmly packed brown
    sugar
2 teaspoons all-purpose flour
dash of salt
2 cups milk
2 tablespoons light corn syrup

2 1/2 cups peeled, sliced
    peaches, mashed
1 tablespoon lemon juice
1/4 cup sugar
1 teaspoon real vanilla
1/2 teaspoon almond extract
1 cup cream

Add lemon juice to mashed peaches to prevent darkening. Beat eggs at medium speed of electric mixer until frothy. Gradually add sugar, brown sugar, flour and salt; beat well. Stir in milk and syrup. Cook over low heat until mixture begins to thicken, stirring constantly. Remove from heat. Chill thoroughly.

Stir peaches into custard. Add flavorings.

Beat cream until soft peaks form; fold into custard mixture

Pour mixture into ice cream maker. Freeze according to manufacturer's instructions. Let ripen at least 1 hour before serving.

Easy Ice Cream Cookies

Makes 5 dozen

1 cup shortening
1 cup sugar
2 eggs, beaten
1 1/2 cup flour

1 teaspoon salt
1 teaspoon real vanilla
1 cup pecan halves

Preheat oven to 325 degrees. Cream shortening; gradually add sugar, beating until light and fluffy. Add eggs, beat well.

Combine flour and salt; add to creamed mixture, beating well. Stir in vanilla.

Drop batter by teaspoonfuls onto greased baking sheets. Press a pecan half in center of each cookie. Bake for 10 minutes or until lightly browned. Cool slightly on baking sheets; remove to wire racks, and let cool completely.

SOUTHERN FRIED PORK CHOPS DINNER

Southern Fried Pork Chops with Gravy
Real Mashed Potatoes
"Don't Stir the Pot" Green Beans
Fried Apples
Geba's Famous Biscuits
Liquid Gold Gingerbread

Southern Fried Pork Chops with Gravy

Our family loves pork and the chops are the girls favorites. They all find time to sit down and eat for this meal.

Serves 6

12 small thinly sliced fresh pork chops	salt
flour for dredging plus 3 tablespoons for gravy	pepper
3 tablespoons vegetable oil or saved drippings	1 cup water/1 cup milk, combined

Dredge each chop in flour, shake off excess. Fry in large skillet in hot oil, turn when brown. Cover and let cook at medium heat until tender. Just before chops are done, about 15 minutes, remove lid and crisp up. Remove and keep warm while making gravy.

Heat drippings in skillet to make 2 tablespoons. Add 3 tablespoons flour, whisk and add milk-water mixture all at once and cook until desired thickness. Salt and pepper to taste. Serve gravy separately.

Real Mashed Potatoes, see page 58 .

"Don't Stir the Pot" Green Beans, see page 58 .

Fried Apples

Use a good quality, tart cooking apple. Delicious with pork breakfast, lunch or dinner.

6 servings

6 apples, large, cored, peeled, cut into eighths, washed (leave water clinging to apples)	4 tablespoons fresh bacon drippings (butter may be substituted but will be different flavor)
1/2 to 1 cup sugar	

Heat shortening in skillet, add apples. Shake pan to gild apples. Scatter sugar over top, cover pan. Cook over low heat until tender, sugar is melted and forms a transparent coating on apples. Raise heat if more color is desired on apples. DO NOT STIR and DO NOT OVERCOOK!

Geba's Famous Biscuits, see page 59 .

Liquid Gold Gingerbread

Travis loves molasses. Each Christmas my parents give Travis a gallon from the new crop, made by the Mennonites in Tennessee using the old, natural process. A gallon is never cheap and always comes in a plain gold pail, thus the name liquid gold.

9 servings

1/2 cup butter	1/2 teaspoon salt
1/2 cup sugar	1 teaspoon cinnamon
2 eggs	1/2 teaspoon ground cloves
1 cup molasses (preferably	1 tablespoon powdered ginger
unsulfured, sorghum)	1 1/2 teaspoon baking soda
2 1/2 cups flour	1 cup hot water

Preheat oven to 350 degrees. Cream butter and sugar in mixer, add eggs, cream well, add molasses. Stir in all dry ingredients that have been sifted together and add hot water last. Beat until smooth. Grease and flour 9 x 9 x 2 inch pan. Smooth batter in pan. Bake 35 minutes. Serve warm with sweetened whipped cream.

1 tablespoon chopped, candied ginger can be added to batter before baking.

Also good served with **Caramel Sauce** see page 38.

Floral Bouquet

COUNTRY FRIED STEAK DINNER

Country Fried Steak
Sawmill Gravy
Iron Skillet Fried Potatoes
Carmelized Tomatoes
Country Corn Relish

Geba's Famous Biscuits
Chess Pie
Buttermilk Pie

Country Fried Steak

Serves 6

6 6-ounce pieces top round, 1/2 inch thick, all fat completely trimmed off.	salt pepper ground red pepper
1 cup flour	shortening for frying
1 cup butermilk	Sawmill Gravy

Score steaks 1/8 inch deep on both sides. Pound steaks with edge of saucer or meat mallet to 1/4-inch thickness. Dredge in flour, shake off excess, dip in buttermilk, redredge in flour.

Heat shortening 1/4 to 1/2 inch in heavy skillet; fry steak 3 to 5 minutes on each side. Salt, pepper and red pepper to taste on each side. Keep warm in oven while making gravy.

Sawmill Gravy

Makes 1 quart

1/2 cup drippings left in skillet (add more shortening if necessary)	2 cups water salt pepper
1/2 cup all purpose flour	tabasco
2 cups milk	

Heat drippings until smoking hot. Add flour and whisk constantly until light brown color. Add milk water mixture. Stir until thickened, add salt, pepper, and tabasco to taste.

Iron Skillet Fried Potatoes

These are great with any country dish as well as hamburgers and steak.

Serves 6

6 medium-sized Idaho
  potatoes
6 tablespoons bacon
  drippings, beef drippings,
  shortening or butter

salt
freshly ground black
  pepper

Peel and thinly slice potatoes. Drop in cold salted water. Drain, pat dry. Heat 12-inch skillet, add oil and heat until almost smoking. Add potatoes, cover and cook at medium-high heat until brown. Turn potatoes over and brown on other side. Return lid, cook until done. A few minutes before they finish cooking, remove cover and let potatoes dry out. Sprinkle with salt and pepper. Serve immediately.

Use food processor to thinly slice potatoes.

Buttermilk Pie

This is a Southern specialty, not too sweet and a little tart.

Serves 6

3 eggs
3/4 cup sugar
3 tablespoons flour
3 tablespoons melted butter
  (no substitutes)
1 1/2 cup fresh buttermilk
1 teaspoon real vanilla extract

3 tablespoons fresh lemon
  juice
grated rind 1 lemon (yellow
  part only)
freshly grated nutmeg
1 9-inch uncooked pastry shell

Preheat oven to 450 degrees. Prick pie shell surface with fork all over to prevent blistering of dough. Bake for 10 minutes in hot oven (DO NOT BROWN.) Remove, let cool

Beat eggs and sugar in mixer until light and lemon colored; add flour, beat. Add rest of ingredients except nutmeg and pour into baked pie shell. Reduce oven to 375 degrees. Dust top of pie with nutmeg, return to oven and bake until filling just sets (DO NOT OVERCOOK), about 20 minutes. Serve warm or at room temperature.

Carmelized Tomatoes

Unusual and delicious

Serves 6

6 firm, ripe, medium homegrown tomatoes, peeled

Caramel Sauce:

2 stalks celery, finely chopped
or ground
1/2 green pepper, finely
chopped or ground
1 medium onion, finely
chopped or ground
6 teaspoons butter
salt to taste

pepper to taste
1 1/2 cups dark brown sugar
1 cup water or juice from
tomatoes
1 heaping tablespoon flour
1 tablespoon fresh lemon
juice

Preheat oven to 375 degrees. Dip each tomato in boiling water. Leave for one to two minutes. Plunge into cold water. Peel. Remove hard core and blossom end. Put one teaspoon of butter in each core hollow and bake in lightly buttered pan for 20 minutes. Save accumulated liquid for Caramel Sauce. Combine ground vegetables and liquid. Heat in saucepan until tender. Add sugar, salt, pepper, and flour mixed with 2 tablespoons cold water to make a paste. Cook until thick, pour over each tomato.

Use food processor to grind vegetables quickly.

Country Corn Relish

When my father's garden was in full production, we would can many relishes, pickles and homemade sauerkraut. This is an easy version which can be kept in the refrigerator.

Makes 1 quart

2 cups whole kernel yellow corn
1 cup finely chopped green cabbage
1 red sweet pepper, finely chopped
2 cups finely chopped celery
1 medium onion, finely chopped

1 clove garlic, minced
1 teaspoon celery seeds
1/2 tablespoon salt
1/2 tablespoon dry mustard
1/2 teaspoon tumeric
dash ground red pepper
1/2 cup sugar
1 cup cider vinegar

In a large saucepan combine all ingredients except vinegar. Blend well and stir in vinegar. Bring to boil, reduce heat, and simmer 15 minutes. DO NOT OVERCOOK. If liquid needs to thicken, drain and boil separately for a few minutes, then add back to vegetables. Chill.

Use food processor to chop vegetables.

Can be processed in hot sterlized jars and sealed according to safe canning procedures.

Geba's Famous Biscuits, see page 59.

Chess Pie

Easy and always good!

Makes 6 rich servings

1/2 cup butter, softened
1 1/2 cups sugar
1 1/2 teaspoon cornmeal (white, finely ground)
1 teaspoon vinegar

2 teaspoons real vanilla extract
3 eggs
1 unbaked 9-inch pie shell

Preheat oven to 425 degrees. Cream butter and sugar until light and fluffy in mixer. Add cornmeal, vinegar, and vanilla, mixing well. Beat in eggs, one at a time. Pour into pie shell. Bake at 425 degrees for 10 minutes; reduce to 350 degrees and bake an additional 20 to 30 minutes, until pie is firm.

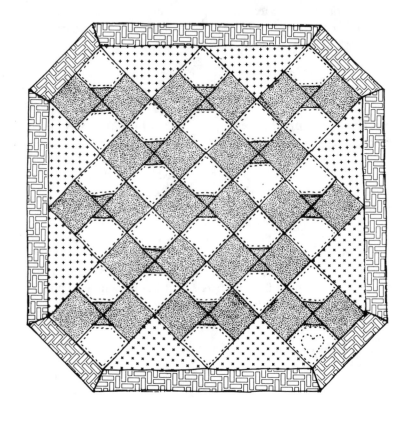

Bow Tie

NEW YEAR'S INTIMATE "BLACK-TIE" DINNER

Champagne
Caviar and Blini
Bleu Cheese Salad
Veal Heart in Hand
Toasted Herb Bread
Divine Chocolate Apricot Roll

Caviar and Blini

Elegant and grand!

Makes approximately 35

1 package dry yeast
1/2 cup warm water
1 cup milk
1 1/2 cups flour
3 egg yolks

1/2 teaspoons salt
sugar
6 tablespoons butter, melted
4 ounces good caviar

Mix first 8 ingredients in food processor. Beat egg whites until stiff, fold into first mixture. Bake by dropping a tablespoon of mixture onto a hot greased griddle, turn once. To serve, place a dollop of sour cream, a finely chopped onion, caviar (good quality) and a fresh dill sprig on top of each blini.

Caviar can also be served on good quality heart toasts. Cut good quality bread with small heart cookie cutter. Bake in a 300-degree oven until dry (DO NOT BROWN). Turn after five minutes to prevent edges curling. Can be stored in tightly covered container. Recrisp before using.

Bleu Cheese Salad

This salad is wonderful. Be sure and use a mixture of good salad greens.

Makes 1 large individual salad

green mixed lettuce
5 ounces good quality bleu
    cheese

1/3 cups pecans, toasted
ripe tomato wedges
sweet red onion rings

Tear enough mixed greens to fill 1 salad plate or bowl. Top with bleu cheese and pecans. Garnish with tomato wedges and onion rings, drizzle Vinaigrette Dressing on top. If smaller dinner salad is in order, decrease the amount of ingredients.

Vinaigrette Dressing

1 tablespoon dijon mustard
4 tablespoons red/wine
    vinegar
2 teaspoons sugar
1/2 teaspoon salt

1/2 teaspoon cracked black
    pepper
1 tablespoon parsley
1/2 to 1 cup good quality
    olive oil

Mix in food processor and taste (adjust only if necessary.)

This makes a great luncheon salad, preceded by a soup, good bread, and followed with a rich dessert.

Veal Heart in Hand

Almost a stew, but quickly cooked. Delicious year 'round.

Makes 4 generous servings

2 pounds veal scallops
(thinly sliced best quality
veal)
flour for dredging
4 tablespoons olive oil
(good quality)
2 tablespoons finely chopped
garlic
2 tablespoons instant chicken
granules or very, very rich
cooked chicken broth

1/2 cup chopped green onions
3 cups sliced mushrooms
including stems
1 1/2 pound canned diced
tomatoes
1 cup good quality white
wine
1 teaspoon black pepper
1 teaspoon thyme
(2 teaspoons, fresh)
2 tablespoons sugar, or to taste

Dredge veal in flour, shake off excess. In large skillet, saute in olive oil. Remove veal. Add all other ingredients to skillet, cook down until wine is reduced (about 5 to 10 minutes). Return veal to pan. Simmer to meld flavors, about 10 to 15 more minutes. Garnish with chopped green parsley and serve with Herb Toasted French Bread.

Toasted Herb Bread, see page 31.

Divine Chocolate Apricot Roll

This really is divine.

Serves 10

Filling

1/2 pound dried apricots, chopped

2 cups water

2 (3-inch) strips lemon peel finely chopped

1/2 cup sugar

3 tablespoons brandy or orange liqueur

1 teaspoons fresh lemon juice

1 tablespoons chopped candied ginger

Cake

8 ounces semisweet chocolate

1/3 cup strong coffee

1 tablespoon instant coffee granules dissolved in coffee

2 teaspoons vanilla

7 egg yolks, room temperature

3/4 cup sugar

8 egg whites, room temperature

Unsweetened cocoa powder

Filling: Combine apricots, water and lemon peel in large saucepan and simmer over medium-low heat until fruit is barely tender, about 10 minutes. Stir in sugar and continue simmering until fruit is tender, about 5 minutes. Remove from heat, mash to a puree. Blend in brandy and lemon juice. Cover and chill.

Cake: Preheat oven to 350 degrees. Grease 11x15-inch jelly roll pan. Line bottom with waxed paper, extending paper over short ends. Grease paper. Combine chocolate and coffee in medium saucepan and warm over very low heat until chocolate melts. Remove from heat. Stir in vanilla, set aside to cool.

Combine yolks and sugar in medium bowl and beat until pale and light. Stir into cooled chocolate mixture. Beat whites in large bowl until stiff but not dry. Gently stir 1/3 of whites into chocolate mixture, then fold chocolate mixture into remaining whites. Pour into prepared pans. Bake 10 minutes. Reduce oven temperature to 300 degrees and continue baking 5 minutes. Remove pan from oven.

Lay large towel on a flat surface and dust with cocoa. Loosen cake around edges with knife and turn out onto towel. Carefully remove paper. Cut off any crisp edges with knife and discard. Beginning on long side, gently roll up cake and towel. (Towel prevents cake from sticking to itself.) Transfer to rack and cool completely.

To assemble: Unroll cake and remove cloth. Spread apricot filling evenly over cake, leaving 1-inch border on all sides. Carefully roll cake up lengthwise. Transfer roll to serving dish. Sift cocoa powder lightly over top. Serve with dollop of apricot brandy whipped cream.

After cake is assembled it can be refrigerated for several hours or frozen. If refrigerated, let stand at room temperature for 1 hour before garnishing and serving.

Can also be filled with pineapple:

2 cups crushed pineapple,
drained
1/2 cup sugar
5 egg yolks

1/2 cup butter
2 tablespoons good quality
orange or apricot liqueur

Puree in food processor. Cook over low heat until thick (put liqueur in after heating.) Chill

Apricot Brandy Whipped Cream

1 cup chilled heavy cream
4 tablespoons sugar

4 tablespoons apricot brandy

Beat cream, sugar and brandy until medium-stiff peaks form.

NEW YEAR'S DAY OPEN HOUSE

Celebration Champagne Punch
Baked Tennessee Country Ham
Geba's Famous Biscuits
Herb Stuffed Mushrooms
Hot Crab-Artichoke Dip
T'NT Black Eyed Peas
Caviar Mousse–Salmon Mousse
Pepper Jelly Turnovers
Brandied Chicken Liver Pate
Tomatoes Stuffed with Avocado
Swedish Meatballs
Elegant English Trifle
Assortment Holiday Desserts

Celebration Champagne Punch

Makes about 5 quarts

1 large fresh ripe pineapple
1 pint firm fresh strawberries
1 pound superfine sugar
1 cup strained fresh lemon
   juice
1 cup strained fresh orange
   juice
1/2 cup curacao or other
   orange-flavored liqueur

1/2 cup brandy
2 quarts champagne, chilled
1 1/2 quarts (6 cups) ginger
   ale, chilled
A (2 to 3 gallon) punch bowl
Ice Ring (ginger ale, orange
   and lemon slices frozen in a
   pretty mold)

Place the pineapple on its side on a cutting board and, grasping it firmly with one hand, slice off the leafy crown and the base with a large sharp knife. Stand the pineapple on end and slice off the prickly rind in seven or eight downward strokes, cutting deep enough each time to remove the eyes. Then divide the fruit lengthwise into quarters and cut the triangular section of core away from each quarter. Cut two of the quarters lengthwise in half and slice each of these crosswise into 1/2-inch-thick wedges. Grate the remaining two quarters of the pineapple on the teardrop-shaped holes of a stand-up hand grater. Set aside the pineapple wedges and grated pineapple.

Pick over the strawberries carefully, removing the stems and hulls and discarding any fruit that is badly bruised or shows signs of mold. Wash briefly in a sieve or colander set under cold running water, then spread the berries on paper towels to drain and pat them completely dry with fresh paper towels.

Just before serving, combine the superfine sugar, lemon and orange juice, curacao and brandy in the punch bowl and stir to dissolve the sugar completely. Stir in the champagne and ginger ale. Carefully place the ice ring in the bowl, then stir the pineapple wedges, grated pineapple and strawberries into the punch.

Baked Tennessee Country Ham

Each state has different methods for raising and curing hams. Our favorite ham is from Tennessee; they are less salty and milder than many other hams. Country ham is one of the favorite entrees in the restaurant.

1 whole country ham

To prepare the ham: Scrub ham thoroughly with a stiff brush to remove all mold and dirt. Soak in water 12 hours or overnight.

Glaze

Whole cloves	1 teaspoon mustard (dry)
2 tablespoons honey	1 tablespoon vinegar
or molasses	Few tablespoons of orange
1 1/2 cups brown sugar	or pineapple juice

Mix above ingredients.

Foil Method: Place ham in a large boat shaped piece of heavy duty foil on a broiling pan (a pan to catch liquid should the "boat" burst). Put 4 cups of water in boat around the ham. Take another piece of heavy duty foil and crimp edges around ham, *making completely airtight.* Place in oven at 400 degrees. When oven reaches 400 degrees bake for 20 minutes. Turn down oven to 250 - 275 degrees. Bake an additional 3 hours or place in 400-degree oven for 45 minutes. Shut off heat. DO NOT PEAK. LEAVE OVERNIGHT.

Prepare for Glazing. When ham has cooled, drain water, cut off all excess fat, leaving a nicely shaped layer of fat on top to score in symmetrical diamond pattern. Place whole cloves in corners of diamond pattern. Brush ham glaze over ham and bake at 325 degrees for 30 minutes.

The hock may be sawed off before cooking to make a more attractive appearance.

Geba's Famous Biscuits, see page 59.

Herb Stuffed Mushrooms, see page 186.

Hot Crab - Artichoke Dip, see page 185.

T'NT Black Eyed Peas, see page 208.

Caviar Mousse

Serves 8

1 cup good quality or
  homemade mayonnaise
1/2 cup sour cream
5 large eggs, hard-boiled and
  grated
3 tablespoons finely grated
  onion
1 1/2 teaspoons Worcestershire

2 tablespoons lemon juice
1/3 teaspoon cayenne pepper
4-ounce jar black lumpfish
  caviar
1 envelope unflavored gelatin
1/4 cup cold water
4-ounce jar red lumpfish
  caviar

Combine mayonnaise, sour cream, eggs and seasonings. Gently fold in caviar. Sprinkle gelatin on cold water. Heat to dissolve. Cool slightly and fold into caviar mixture thoroughly. Pour into lightly oiled 3 1/2 cup mold. Chill at least 4 hours. Unmold and garnish with red caviar on top. Serve with white and whole wheat toast points.

Encircle the mold with bright green parsley or watercress.

Double or triple this for a large gathering.

Salmon Mousse

Serves 12

Court Bouillon

4 cups water
1/4 cup vermouth
wedge of lemon
1 small onion

1 bay leaf
1 teaspoon salt
3 peppercorns

Mousse

2 pounds fresh salmon,
  poached
2 tablespoons gelatin
  (unflavored)
2 tablespoons grated onion
1/4 cup lemon juice
1/3 cup mayonnaise
1/2 cup sour cream

1/2 teaspoon freshly grated
  nutmeg
1 teaspoon salt
1/4 teaspoon freshly ground
  pepper
3/4 cup heavy cream
2 tablespoons chopped
  fresh dill.

In a large pot, combine all court bouillon ingredients and simmer 10 minutes. Place salmon in court bouillon. Bring to a gentle boil, reduce heat and simmer, covered, 10 to 15 minutes, or until salmon flakes easily with fork. Remove from heat and cool salmon in liquid. Strain poaching liquid and set aside.

When Salmon has cooled, remove skin and all bones carefully. Break fish into small pieces with fingers and add 1/2 cup reserved stock.

In a small bowl, soften gelatin in lemon juice.

In a saucepan, bring 1 cup reserved stock to boil. Add gelatin mixture and stir until dissolved. Set aside to cool.

In a large bowl, combine salmon, gelatin mixture, onions, mayonnaise, sour cream, nutmeg, sat, and pepper. Mix together gently but thoroughly. Beat cream until stiff. Fold into salmon mixture.

Oil a ring mold or loaf pan with 6 cup capacity. Carefully spoon mousse into mold. Cover and refrigerate to set.

To serve, invert salmon mousse on serving tray until it unmolds. Garnish with dill and lemon wedges.

Pepper Jelly Turnovers

A delightful surprise.

Makes approximately 16 turnovers

1 (5-ounce) jar Old English
 Cheese
1/2 cup butter
2 tablespoons water

1 cup flour
1 (4-ounce) jar pepper
 jelly

Preheat oven to 375 degrees.

Combine cheese, butter, water and flour to make pastry. Refrigerate overnight.

Roll out dough 1/4 inch thick, cut out circles with 2-inch biscuit cutter. Put 1/4 teaspoon jelly in center, fold over, crimp edges with fork. Bake at 375 degrees for 10 minutes.

Can be frozen, keeps well. Reheat before serving.

Brandied Chicken Liver Pate

Unusual and delicious

Serves 10

10 tablespoons butter
1/2 cup onion, minced
2 small apples, peeled, cored
 and diced
1 pound chicken livers
3 tablespoons brandy
1 1/2 teaspoons lemon juice

2 tablespoons heavy cream
1 teaspoon curry powder, or
 to taste
salt and pepper to taste
1/2 cup raisins
1 tablespoon chopped
 candied ginger

Melt 6 tablespoons butter in a heavy skillet over high heat. When foam subsides, add onion and apple. Saute until apple is soft enough to be mashed with a spoon. Pour contents of skillet into a blender. In skillet, melt the remaining butter and livers. Cook over high heat until the livers are browned, about 5 minutes. Add brandy and flame. When the flame subsides pour the contents into the blender with the apples and onion. Add cream and blend until smooth. Add seasonings and blend about 30 seconds more. Pour the mixture out and shape into a mound. Surround with parsley and serve with thinly sliced French bread.

A good keeper to have on hand.

Tomatoes Stuffed with Avocado

Makes approximately 30-32

2 pints cherry tomatoes
2 ripe avocados
Lime juice to taste
Salt and pepper to taste

1 small minced onion
1 small clove garlic, finely
minced

Core the tomatoes and place upside down to drain. Mash avocados with rest of ingredients. Spoon or pipe with star tube and pastry bag into each tomato. Chill and serve.

Swedish Meat Balls

Everyone loves a good meatball, especially in a rich sauce!

Serves 30

3 cups soft bread crumbs
2 cups half and half
3 pounds ground round
3 eggs, well beaten
6 tablespoons minced onion
1 teaspoon mace
1/2 teaspoon allspice
3 teaspoons salt
1 teaspoon pepper
oil

8 tablespoons flour
3 (10 1/2 ounce) cans
condensed consomme or
rich brown broth
1 cup dry white wine
2 cups heavy cream
4 tablespoons chopped parsley
4 tablespoons chopped
fresh dill

Soak bread crumbs in milk. Saute minced onion in a little butter until tender but not brown, Combine bread crumbs, onion, ground round, beaten eggs, mace, allspice, salt and pepper. Mix thoroughly. With wet hands shape meat mixture into balls the size of a walnut. Heat oil and brown meat balls on all sides. Remove balls and stir flour into oil. Add consomme, wine and cream. Stir constantly until sauce is thick and smooth. Return balls to gravy, cover skillet and let simmer for 20 minutes or place meatballs and gravy in ovenproof casserole until heated through. Serve in chafing dish for buffet.

After meatballs and gravy are completely done, 1 cup of sour cream can be added for a tangy flavor.

Elegant English Trifle

This is a wonderful recipe to use up leftover cake, cookies, and Christmas custard or to make just because it is so delicious! Be sure and use a beautiful bowl and garnish with red and green for the holiday season.

Serves 8-10

2 cups Old Fashioned
  Christmas Custard
1 teaspoon unflavored gelatin
1 layer Christmas Coconut
  Cake, iced or plain, or 2
  dozen ladyfingers, split
1 cup Red Raspberry Jam
1 cup dry sherry
4 tablespoons brandy

Ambrosia or fresh seasonal
  fruits
1 dozen Macaroons, crushed
  and divided
2 cups whipping cream,
  whipped
1/2 cup almonds, slivered
  and toasted

Gently heat custard, add gelatin.

Cut cake into finger length pieces. Coat 1/2 of the pieces with 1/2 of the raspberry jam. Place in bottom of an 8 inch in diameter crystal or clear bowl at least 3 1/2 inches deep.

Sprinkle with 1/2 the sherry and brandy.

Cover with a layer of ambrosia and 1/2 of the macaroons. Repeat with layers of 1/2 the custard, cake, jam, sherry, brandy, ambrosia, and remaining macaroons. Repeat custard layer. Chill.

Just before serving, top with whipped cream and almonds.

Macaroons

Makes about 3 dozen

16 ounces blanched almonds,
  finely chopped
1 tablespoon almond extract

3 egg whites
3 cups sifted powdered sugar

Preheat oven to 300 degrees. Combine almonds and almond extract. Set aside.

Beat egg whites (at room temperature) until foamy, gradually add sugar, beating until stiff peaks form. Fold in almond mixture. Drop mixture by heaping teaspoons onto unglazed brown paper on cookie sheet. Bake for 30 minutes or until lightly browned. Remove from paper with spatula while warm. Two cups grated coconut may be substituted for the almonds to make coconut macaroons.

VALENTINE'S DINNER

Clifton Sunset

Heart Cheese Straws

Duck Breast in Gingered Brown Sauce

Oven Baked Wild Rice

Sauteed Fresh Vegetable Medley

Heart Meringues with

Heart in Hand Raspberry Ice Cream

Fudge Sauce

Clifton Sunset

As pretty as a sunset. A pretty way to start off a romantic meal.

Serves 10

1 #3 can cranberry juice
1 12 ounce can frozen
   limeade concentrate
12 ounces Southern Comfort

3 lemons, sliced or halved
3 limes, sliced or halved
3 oranges, sliced or halved.

Combine above liquids. Add fruits that have been halved or sliced and muddled (mashed with spoon) to extract juices. Pour into pitcher or container. Stays refrigerated for a long time. When serving, garnish each glass with a fresh slice of lemon, lime and orange and a sprig of mint.

Heart Cheese Straws, see page 23.

Sauteed Fresh Vegetable Medley, see page 20.

Duck Breast in Gingered Brown Sauce

We get raves on this one, I'm sure you'll enjoy it too.

Serves 6

6 boneless duck breasts	1/2 cup rum
1 cup lemon juice	1 1/2 tablespoons cracked
1/2 cup lime juice	black pepper
1/2 cup brown sugar	

Mix the marinade ingredients and marinate duck breasts overnight turning occasionally. Make Gingered Brown Sauce.

Gingered Brown Sauce

Makes 4 cups

1 onion	1/2 cup strong coffee
2 carrots	1 cup red wine
2 stalks celery	1/4 cup port
1/2 cup butter	ginger to taste
3/4 cup flour	sugar to taste
2 bay leaves	salt to taste
2 cloves garlic	pepper to taste
2 cans beef consomme (5 cups)	

Chop vegetables fine, melt in butter, add flour, brown, whisk in all liquid ingredients. Add bay leaves and seasonings to taste. Simmer 2 or 3 hours until it becomes a really rich brown sauce. Taste. Adjust seasonings. You want a pronounced ginger flavor with a hint of sweetness.

When ready to roast, preheat oven to 450 degrees; prick skin on breasts, to release fat. Roast breasts for 10 minutes. Turn down to 400 degrees and continue for 20 minutes. Check for doneness. DO NOT OVERCOOK. Duck is best medium rare. Let set for a few minutes. Slice in thin slices.

To Serve

Place a pool of Gingered Brown Sauce on a plate, place duck slices in a fan pattern over sauce. Garnish with watercress and an orange half or twist.

Oven Baked Wild Rice

For Oven Baked Wild Rice use same recipe as for Oven Baked Rice (page 31) substituting wild rice for white rice.

Meringue Hearts

Makes 6

1/2 cup egg whites
1/8 teaspoon salt
3/4 cup sugar

1/2 teaspoon real vanilla
   extract

Preheat oven to 300 degrees. Combine egg whites and salt; beat with electric mixer at high speed until stiff. Add sugar, 1 tablespoon at a time, beating well after each addition. Stir in vanilla. Draw 6 (4-inch) hearts on heavy brown paper, place on cookie sheet. Spoon meringue in mounds onto heart outlines. Make deep well in center of each mound, building up sides with back of spoon to form hearts. Bake until meringues are delicate golden color, 12 to 15 minutes. Lower heat to 250 degrees; continue baking until dry and light brown in color, 30 to 40 minutes. Turn off heat, leave shells in oven with door closed for 1 to 2 hours. Remove from oven to cool completely. (Shells may be frozen. Store in airtight container. Return unfilled shells to oven to crisp lightly before filling.) Place 1 rounded scoop Heart in Hand Raspberry Ice Cream into each shell, drizzle chocolate sauce on top.

Heart in Hand Raspberry Ice Cream, see page 32.

Fudge Sauce

Simple but good!

Makes 2 cups

6 ounces semisweet chocolate,
   chopped (use best quality)

2 cups heavy cream

Add chocolate to the cream and melt over low heat, stirring constantly. Cool until thickened. Serve hot or cold. Stores well in refrigerator.

St. Valentine's Patch,
also called Double Hearts

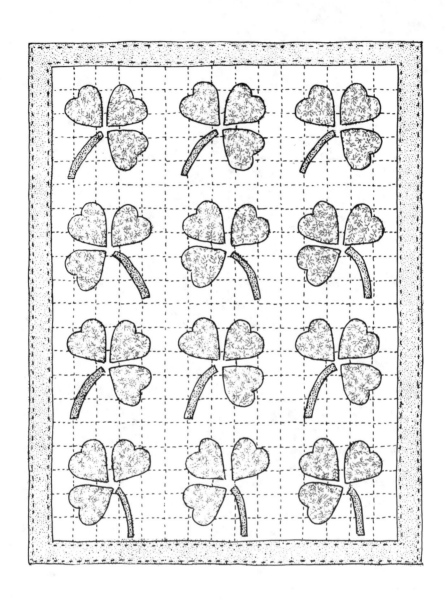

Shamrock Applique

St. PADDY'S DAY IN CLIFTON

Traditional Corned Beef Dinner
Horseradish Cream
Irish Soda Bread
Grasshopper Pie
Irish Coffee

Traditional Corned Beef Dinner

Serves 8 to 10

1 (4 to 5) pound corned beef
brisket, trimmed
2 bay leaves
1 1/2 teaspoons whole cloves
1 1/2 teaspoons whole
peppercorns
1 medium cabbage, cut into
wedges

6 medium potatoes, peeled
and cubed
6 medium carrots, scraped
and cut in julienne strips
4 medium onions, peeled and
quartered
Fresh parsley sprigs

Place brisket in a large Dutch oven; cover with water. Add spices. Bring to a boil and cover; reduce heat, simmer for 2 1/2 hours or until brisket is tender.

Add cabbage; cover and simmer 10 minutes. Add potatoes, carrots, and onions; cover and simmer an additional 20 minutes or until vegetables are tender.

Remove brisket to a warm platter; slice thinly across the grain. Remove vegetables from liquid, discarding spices. Place on platter with sliced brisket. Garnish with parsley.

Horseradish Cream

Whip 1/2 pint whipping cream till stiff, add horseradish to taste and a pinch of sugar.

Any leftover corned beef is delicious on the Irish Soda Bread with Kitty Bean's Sandwich Spread.

Kitty Bean's Sandwich Spread

The late Kitty Bean, the first president and founder of the Clifton Community Women's Club, gave me this delightful recipe. Kitty was an enthusiastic, energetic worker, who found time not only to be a good leader, but also to be a good friend.

Yield: 12 pints

12 green peppers	1 cup flour
12 red peppers	1 cup prepared mustard
12 green tomatoes	2 tablespoons salt
2 cups vinegar	1 quart mayonnaise
2 cups sugar	

Chop peppers and tomatoes in food processor. Drain, rinse well and drain again. Mix sugar, flour, tomatoes and peppers, bring to a boil in large pot. Remove from heat and add mayonnaise. Recipe can be halved or quartered and kept in the refrigerator—or brought to boil for a few minutes and processed in hot sterilized jars and sealed according to safe canning procedures.

Irish Soda Bread

This bread is so easy to make. It's delicious warm with a crock of whipped butter.

Yield: 1 loaf

4 cups all-purpose flour	1 cup seedless raisins
1/4 cup sugar	1 1/3 cups buttermilk
1 teaspoon salt	1 egg
1 teaspoon baking powder	1 teaspoon baking soda
1/4 cup butter	1 tablespoon caraway seeds

Preheat oven to 375 degrees. Mix flour, sugar, salt and baking powder. Cut in butter until it resembles coarse corn meal. Stir in raisins. Combine buttermilk, egg and soda. Add to flour mixture until just moistened. Bake in greased 1 quart pan until golden, about 45 to 50 minutes.

Grasshopper Pie

Green and minty! Perfect ending for "wearin' of the Green!"

Serves 6-8

Crust

1 1/4 cups chocolate wafer crumbs	1/4 cup sugar 1/3 cup melted butter

Mix ingredients and press against bottom and sides of a 9-inch pie pan. Bake in 400 degree oven for 5 minutes. Cool.

Filling

1 envelope unflavored gelatin	1/4 cup green creme de menthe
1/2 cup sugar	1/4 cup white creme de cacao
dash salt	1 cup heavy cream, whipped
1/2 cup cold water	
3 eggs, separated	

Mix gelatin, 1/4 cup of the sugar and the salt in top of a double boiler. Add water and egg yolks one at a time, blending well. Place over boiling water and stir constantly until gelatin dissolves and mixture thickens slightly, about 5 minutes. Remove from heat; stir in liqueurs. Chill, stirring occasionally, until mixture is consistency of unbeaten egg white. Beat egg whites stiff. Gradually add remaining sugar. Fold into gelatin mixture. Fold in whipped cream. Turn into crumb shell and chill 2 hours or overnight. Garnish with additional whipped cream and shaved chocolate.

Irish Coffee

Dip rim of glass in water and roll in sugar.

Serves 1

1 1/2 ounces Irish Whisky	green creme de menthe
1 heaping teaspoon sugar	maraschino cherry and mint
coffee	leaf for garnish
stiff whipped cream	

Into a stemmed glass or cup pour Irish Whisky, fill to within 1/2 inch of top with strong hot black coffee. Add stiff whipped cream, drizzle green creme de menthe on top. Garnish with maraschino cherry and mint leaf.

EASTER SUNDAY DINNER

Virginia Peanut Soup
Celebration Baked Ham
Brandied Peaches

Garlic Roasted Leg of Lamb
Brandied Peaches or
English Lamb Sauce
Whipped White Potatoes
Country Asparagus Casserole
Geba's Pickled Beets
Clover Leaf Rolls
Lemon Meringue Pie
Springtime Fresh Strawberry Pie

Virginia Peanut Soup

Rich and creamy, this soup is a tradition in Virginia and a favorite at the restaurant in any season.

Serves 8

2 quarts chicken broth
1 small onion, diced
1/4 pound butter
2 stalks celery, diced
3 tablespoons flour
2 cups peanut butter

1/2 cup ground Virginia
  peanuts
1/3 teaspoon celery salt
1 teaspoon salt
1 tablespoon lemon juice

Melt butter, add onion and celery. Saute for 5 minutes but do not brown. Add flour and blend well. Stir in chicken broth and cook for 30 minutes. Remove from heat, strain. Add peanut butter, celery salt, salt and lemon juice. Sprinkle ground peanuts on soup just before serving.

Celebration Baked Ham, see page 204.

Brandied Peaches

A pretty, tasty accompaniment for the ham or the lamb. It makes a stunning platter when you alternate the peaches with bunches of watercress or mint encircling the meat.

Serves 12

12 coconut macaroons
1 stick butter, melted
1/4 cup pecan halves, coarsely
  chopped in food processor
2 tablespoons brown sugar

4 tablespoons apricot or
  peach brandy
salt
12 canned peach halves

Preheat oven to 300 degrees. Place peach halves in muffin tin (to help keep their shape.) Fill each cavity with a macaroon and pecans. Combine butter, sugar, brandy and salt and drizzle on top of each peach and heat for 15 minutes.

Garlic Roasted Leg of Lamb

A spring tradition. I love to smell the garlic aroma when the lamb is cooking.

Serves 4 to 6

4 to 6 pound leg of lamb
(good quality spring lamb)
5 to 7 garlic cloves, slivered
1 cup honey

1/4 cup fresh lemon juice
1 tablespoon oregano
1 tablespoon grated lemon
peel

Preheat oven to 325 degrees. Make 10 to 15 pockets in meat by piercing with knife tip. Insert garlic sliver in each pocket. Mix honey, lemon juice, oregano and lemon peel together and use as basting sauce. Roast lamb uncovered at 325 for 35 minutes per pound. Baste frequently. DO NOT OVERCOOK LAMB.

English Lamb Sauce

Makes 2 1/2 cups

1 cup sugar
2 cups tarragon vinegar
1 cup water
1/2 teaspoon mint extract

1 tablespoon chopped
tarragon
2 tablespoons chopped green
onion.

Put all ingredients in 2-quart saucepan. Boil rapidly to reduce down until sugar dissolves and flavors mingle, and to reduce mixture into a thin syrupy sauce.

Pepper Jelly Mint Sauce

Mix equal amounts of pepper and mint jellies. Add finely chopped fresh mint to taste.

Whipped White Potatoes

Everyone loves creamy white mashed potatoes.

Serves 6

6 medium-sized potatoes	1/2 teaspoon freshly ground
1 teaspoon salt	white pepper
1/2 cup butter	1 cup hot milk

Wash and pare the potatoes and cut them in half. Place them in a saucepan and pour in boiling water to cover. Add the salt and cook briskly for 20 minutes.

Drain and mash with a potato masher. Add the butter, pepper, and salt to taste. Pour in the hot milk and beat well by hand or with an electric mixer until the potatoes are light and fluffy.

Country Asparagus Casserole

This has "old-timey" good taste. Always expected on our Easter table.

Serves 8

3 cups cooked asparagus, cut into 1-inch pieces	2 teaspoons salt
	1/4 teaspoon pepper
1 cup chopped onion	4 hard-cooked eggs, sliced
1/4 cup butter	1/2 cup shredded Cheddar
6 tablespoons flour	cheese
3 cups milk	1/2 cup dry bread crumbs

Preheat oven to 350 degrees. In a large skillet, cook onion in butter until tender (not brown). Stir in flour. Add milk and cook, stirring constantly, until thickened. Mix in salt, pepper, eggs and asparagus.

Turn into a 2-quart casserole. Top with cheese and crumbs. Bake for 30 minutes, until hot and bubbly.

Geba's Pickled Beets, see page 209.

Mildred's Southern Rolls

One recipe of Mildred's Southern Rolls, page 209.

For Cloverleafs

Shape dough in long rolls 1 inch in diameter. Cut off 1-inch pieces and form each into a small ball. Place 3 balls in each greased muffin-pan cup. Balls should touch bottom of cups and fill them half full. Brush with melted butter.

For Parkerhouse Rolls

Roll dough 1/4-inch thick on lightly floured board, cut in rounds with 2 1/2-inch floured biscuit or cookie cutter. Brush with melted butter. Make a crease in each round just off center with back of table knife. Fold larger side of each round over other side, overlapping slightly. Seal end edges. Brush with melted butter, place rolls about 1 inch apart on greased baking sheet.

Follow rising and baking instructions on page 209.

Lemon Meringue Pie

A tart dessert, so good after a rich meal.

Makes 1 (9-inch) pie

1 1/2 cups sugar
1/4 cup plus 2 tablespoons
cornstarch
1/4 teaspoon salt
2 cups cold water
1/2 cup lemon juice, fresh
squeezed
3 eggs, separated
2 tablespoons butter

2 teaspoons grated lemon
rind
3 to 4 drops yellow food
coloring
1/4 teaspoon cream of tartar
1/4 cup plus 2 tablespoons
sugar
1 (9-inch) baked pastry shell

Combine 1 1/2 cups sugar, cornstarch, and salt in a large heavy saucepan; mix well. Gradually add water and lemon juice, stirring until mixture is smooth.

Beat egg yolks until thick and lemon colored; gradually stir into lemon mixture. Add butter. Cook over medium heat; stir constantly until thickened and bubbly. Cook 1 minute, stirring constantly. Remove from heat; stir in rind and food coloring. Pour into prepared pastry shell.

Combine egg whites (at room temperature) and cream of tartar; beat until foamy. Gradually add remaining sugar, 1 tablespoon at a time, beating until stiff peaks form. Spread meringue over filling, sealing to edge of pastry. Bake at 350 degrees for 12 to 15 minutes or until golden brown. Cool to room temperature.

Springtime Fresh Strawberry Pie

What could be prettier than a shimmering glazed strawberry pie?

Makes 1 (9-inch) pie

Filling:

1 1/2 to 2 quarts fresh
  strawberries
1 cup water
1 cup sugar

2 tablespoons cornstarch
4 tablespoons strawberry
  flavor gelatin

Mix water, sugar and cornstarch and bring to a boil. Add strawberry jello. Set aside to cool. Fill baked shell with strawberries. Pour cooked mixture over this.

Butter Pecan Crust

1/2 cup butter
1 cup flour

1/4 cup light brown sugar
1/3 cup chopped pecans

Preheat oven to 375 degrees. Blend butter, flour and sugar until crumbs form. Stir in nuts. Press mixture into a 9-inch pie plate. Bake for 12 - 15 minutes until golden brown.

Easter Tide

MOTHER'S DAY DINNER

Mother's Day is the busiest day of the year for us at the restaurant. This is one of the favorite menus used on that day.

Champagne Cocktail

Asparagus with Raspberry Viniagrette

Elegant Seafood Crepes

Herb Baked Tomatoes

Geba's Spoon Rolls

Cold Lemon Souffle

Liqueured Strawberries

Heart in Hand Butter Tea Cookies

Champagne Cocktail

Makes 1

1 lump sugar   **2 dashes Bitters**

Place in champagne glass and fill with chilled champagne. Add a twist of lemon or orange peel.

Asparagus with Raspberry Viniagrette

This is a very pretty dish!
Serves 6

30 asparagus stalks   **1 cup heavy whipping cream**
pinch of baking soda   **1 1/2 teaspoons tarragon**
1 10-ounce box frozen red   **vinegar**
** raspberries, partially thawed**   **Fresh tarragon, only**

Peel asparagus, leaving tip intact, cut off tough wood end. In a large flat skillet, non-stick coated or stainless steel, bring enough water to cover stalks to boil. Add pinch of soda. Add a few stalks at a time so asparagus continues boiling. Cook 2 to 5 minutes ONLY depending on thickness of asparagus. DO NOT OVERCOOK. Plunge into cold water; drain, chill.

Viniagrette: Whirl sauce ingredients in blender or food processor until smooth. Chill.

Leftover vinaigrette can be used on other greens or used in Raspberry Chicken, see page 34.

Geba's Spoon Rolls

Absolutely delicious and easy to make!
Yield: 2 dozen

2 cups warm water   **1/2 cup sugar**
1 tablespoon dry yeast   **3/4 cup light oil**
1 egg (beaten)   **4 cups self-rising flour**

Preheat oven to 400 degrees. Add yeast to warm water, add egg, sugar, oil to yeast water mixture, mix well, then add the flour (mixture will be soupy).

Grease muffin tins with oil or non-stick spray, drop roll mixture to fill 2/3 full. Bake for 8 to 10 minutes.

Elegant Seafood Crepes

The name says it all. A wonderful dish for a special mom!
Serves 12

Crepes:

1 cup cold milk	1 teaspoon salt
1 cup cold water	2 cups flour
4 eggs	4 tablespoons melted butter

Blend all ingredients in blender and store in refrigerator for several hours. Heat 6-7 inch crepe pan and grease with a bit of butter. Pour a scant 1/4 cup batter in pan and swirl until batter covers bottom of pan. Cook until edges brown and lift up to see if brown on bottom. Then turn with a spatula and cook until this side is browned lightly. Place crepe on plate and cover with piece of wax paper. Regrease pan and make the next crepe, stacking cooked crepes on top of each other with a piece of wax paper in between.

Filling:

1 stick butter (no substitute)	dash cayenne pepper
1/2 green onions, minced	1 pound crabmeat
1/4 cup finely chopped green pepper	1 pound medium cooked shrimp
1/4 cup finely chopped pimento	1/2 cup vermouth
	salt and white pepper to taste

For filling, melt butter in large skillet. Combine onion, pepper, pimento, cayenne pepper, salt and pepper, crab and shrimp and toss lightly. Add vermouth and boil rapidly until liquid is almost evaporated. Remove to a bowl and set aside.

Sauce:

2/3 cup dry sherry	4 cups heavy cream
1/4 cup cornstarch	salt and white pepper
1/4 cup milk	2 1/2 cups grated Swiss cheese

For sauce, using the same skillet that filling was cooked in, add dry sherry and boil until reduced to 2 tablespoons. Mix cornstarch and milk and add to dry sherry; heat through. Reduce heat to low and add cream slowly, then add salt and pepper. Thicken slightly and stir in 1 1/2 cups grated cheese. Cook until melted and well-blended. Blend half the sauce with the seafood filling. Put a large spoonful on each crepe and roll up, placing the seam side down in a large buttered rectangular Pyrex baking dish. Spoon remaining sauce over crepes and sprinkle with remaining cheese. Bake 20 minutes at 400 degrees until hot and bubbly; brown under broiler.

Herb Baked Tomatoes

Colorful! Tasty!

Serves 6

6 firm ripe tomatoes,
  3 to 4 inches in diameter
salt
2 cups fresh white bread
  crumbs, not too fine

1/2 cup parsley, finely
  chopped, fresh
1/3 to 1/2 cup Herb Butter

Preheat oven to 375 degrees. Wash and core tomatoes. Scoop out the seeds and sprinkle the insides with salt; turn them upside down to drain. In a large mixing bowl, stir together the bread crumbs, parsley, and Herb Butter (see page 31), but leave it crumbly. Fill each tomato with about 4 tablespoons of the crumb mixture, mounded in the middle. Arrange the tomatoes in a shallow baking dish without crowding them. Sprinkle a few drops of oil over each. Bake in the upper third of oven for 20-30 minutes.

Cold Lemon Souffle

After a rich meal, a lemon dessert is what you need.

Serves 6

1 tablespoon gelatin
1/2 cup water
3 eggs, separated
1 egg white, extra
grated rind of 2 lemons

1 cup sugar
1 teaspoon real vanilla
2 cups heavy cream
1/3 cup freshly squeezed
  lemon juice

Beat yolks with the sugar until pale and thick. Dissolve gelatin in water, melt over hot water, add to eggs. Add lemon juice, vanilla rind. Beat 4 egg whites until stiff. Beat 1 1/2 cups cream until stiff. Fold whites into yolks (one-third first, then the rest.) Fold in whipped cream. Put in 6 pretty stemmed goblets and chill at least 3 hours. Top with dollop of remaining whipped cream, garnish with liqueured strawberry and a mint leaf. Serve with a Heart in Hand Butter Tea Cookie .

Liqueured Strawberries

Delightful surprise to end the meal.

Yield: 12 strawberries

1 cup orange liqueur
(very good quality)

12 extra-large strawberries,
blemish free

Using a plastic medical syringe with a large needle or a basting syringe with needle, draw syringe full of liqueur. Insert needle very close to green hulls of strawberries until end of needle reaches cavity within berry. Gently but firmly push enough liqueur into cavity to fill it.

Heart in Hand Butter Tea Cookie

We have made these by the thousands . . . . and they are always good!

Makes 3 dozen large hearts or 6 dozen tea size hearts.

1 cup butter, softened
(no substitute)
2 cups sugar
3 eggs
1 1/2 tablespoons cream

2 teaspoons real vanilla
4 1/2 cups all-purpose flour
1 tablespoon baking powder
1 1/2 teaspoons salt

Preheat oven to 375 degrees. Cream butter; gradually add sugar, beating well. Add eggs, cream and vanilla, mix well.

Combine dry ingredients; gradually add to creamed mixture, mixing well after each addition. Divide dough in half. Chill dough overnight or in freezer for several hours.

Roll half of dough to 1/4-inch thickness on a lightly floured surface; keep remaining dough chilled. Cut dough with a small heart-shaped cookie cutter. Place on lightly greased baking sheets; bake for 8 to 10 minutes or until edges are lightly browned. Cool on a wire rack. Repeat procedure with remaining dough.

This dough can be made in advance, frozen, used when needed.

Finished cookies may also be frozen.

Trip Around the World

FATHER'S DAY DINNER

This special menu is for Travis, his favorite foods—from the oysters to the cake. The Dad at your house will enjoy this meal too!

Oysters on 1/2 Shell

Best Cocktail Sauce

Herbed Rib Roast of Beef

Rich Madeira Sauce

Garlic Mashed Potatoes

Buttered Green Beans

Never-Fail Popovers

Mother Never Knew German Chocolate Cake

Oysters on 1/2 shell

For oyster lovers, there's nothing better!

Serves 6

36 fresh oysters in shell   cocktail sauce
lemons

Scrub outside shell, run under cold water. Pry open with oyster knife. Serve on lettuce leaf lined plate, 6 per person, with large dollop cocktail sauce in center and lemon wedges for garnish.

Best Cocktail Sauce

Makes 1 generous cup

3/4 cup catsup   Big dash Tabasco
1/4 cup chili sauce   **1/4 cup finely chopped green**
2 tablespoons lemon juice   **onions**
3 tablespoons horseradish   **1 teaspoon Worchestershire**

Combine, chill. Serve with seafood.

Herbed Rib Roast of Beef

A rib roast at our house is always special. The aroma of the fresh herbs and beef cooking fills the house. Everyone can hardly wait.

Serves 8

1 (10 pound) standing rib roast	Black pepper, freshly ground
Thyme, fresh or dried	Ground red pepper
Rosemary, fresh or dried	Garlic powder

This is a good method to cook a standing rib roast so that it will be crusty and brown on the outside and evenly rare and juicy on the inside. The roast must be at room temperature before cooking. Leave it out of the refrigerator 1 hour for each pound of roast.

Do not open the oven door at least for 3 hours after prescribed cooking time is completed. The roast cooks on retained heat.

Season roast by rubbing above herbs on exterior of roast, to taste; and place it rib side down in a shallow pan. Put it uncovered, in a preheated 425 degree oven. Get timer and turn off heat as indicated by the chart below. RESIST THE URGE TO PEEK.

Standing Rib Roast	Temperature: 425 Degrees
5 pounds	35 minutes
6 pounds	40 minutes
7 pounds	45 minutes
8 pounds	50 minutes
9 pounds	55 minutes
10 pounds	1 hour

The roast will have finished cooking but will still be warm even after 4-5 hours, depending on size. If you need the oven, remove the roast and cover with foil to retain heat. Or reheat it if necessary. Never reheat roast beef that has been refrigerated and expect it to taste the same. Do not salt until serving time.

For well-done roast beef use the following method.

Cook a 5 1/2 pound standing rib roast at 425 degrees for 1 hour and 20 minutes and leave it in the oven 4 hours.

Rich Madeira Sauce

Serves 8

3 tablespoons beef drippings or vegetable oil	3 cups strong beef stock
	1/2 cup Madeira
5 tablespoons flour	2 tablespoons butter

In heavy saucepan or skillet, heat oil, add flour, cook on high heat until medium brown in color. Whisk in 3 cups stock, add Madeira, boil until desired thickness, remove from heat; whisk in butter.

This sauce is excellent with steaks or can be used to dress up hamburgers.

Garlic Mashed Potatoes

This is a nice accompaniment for any beef dish. It is not as strong in flavor as you think!

Serves 6

1 recipe Real Mashed Potatoes (page 58); add 1 WHOLE head of garlic, peeled, to the cooking water. Cook with potatoes until done. Drain. Mash garlic in with potatoes.

Buttered Green Beans, see page 63

Never-Fail Popovers

Nothing better than the hot popovers dipped in the Rich Madeira Sauce.

Makes 6

1 cup flour	1 cup milk
1/4 teaspoon salt	1 teaspoon melted butter
2 eggs, slightly beaten	

Sift flour and salt. Combine eggs, milk and butter and stir into dry ingredients, beating until smooth. Divide among 6 well-greased custard cups and place on a cookie sheet in a cold oven. Turn heat to 425 degrees and bake 30 minutes; lower to 350 and bake 20-25 minutes more. Stick point of a sharp knife in popovers immediately to let steam escape. Serve piping hot. They should be puffed and golden brown.

Mother Never Knew—German Chocolate Cake

When I was eleven years old, Mother asked me to prepare this cake for her to take on a plane to my sister and her husband in Michigan. A child being a child, I never got around to making it. Around midnight, I was yanked out of bed to make the cake. In my "sleepy state" I melted the chocolate in too much water. Realizing my mistake, with the chocolate being expensive and the proportion being wrong, I quickly poured the excess down the commode. The cake turned out beautiful. . .a shade lighter, maybe. To this day—MOTHER NEVER KNEW. (Now she does!)

Travis thinks this is the best cake ever! not only is it rich, gooey and chocolate flavored—it's also beautiful to look at, a good keeper, and freezes well too!

1 4-ounce package German sweet baking chocolate	1 cup buttermilk
1/2 cup boiling water	2 1/4 cups all-purpose flour
1 cup butter, softened	1/2 teaspoon salt
2 cups sugar	1 teaspoon real vanilla extract
4 eggs, separated	Coconut-pecan filling
1 teaspoon baking soda	Mocha Frosting

Preheat the oven to 350 degrees. Combine chocolate and boiling water; stir until melted. Set aside. Cream butter, gradually add sugar, beating well. Add egg yolks, one at a time, beating well after each addition. Add chocolate mixture, beat well.

Dissolve soda in buttermilk. Combine flour and salt; add to creamed mixture alternately with buttermilk mixture, beginning and ending with flour mixture. Stir in vanilla.

Beat egg whites (at room temperature) until stiff peaks form; fold into batter. Pour batter into 3 waxed paper-lined and greased 9-inch round cakepans. Bake for 30 minutes or until a wooden pick inserted in center comes out clean. Cool in pans 10 minutes; remove from pans and cool completely.

Coconut-Pecan Filling

Makes enough for one 3-layer cake

1 cup whipping cream
1 cup sugar
3 egg yolks
1/2 cup butter

1 teaspoon real vanilla
1 1/3 cups flaked coconut
1 cup chopped pecans

Combine cream, sugar, egg yolks and butter in a medium sauce pan; cook over medium heat, stirring constantly, until thickened. Remove from heat and stir in vanilla. Stir in remaining ingredients, and let cool completely.

Mocha Frosting

Makes enough for one 3-layer cake

1/2 cup butter, softened
2 tablespoons cocoa
3 tablespoons strong coffee
1 egg yolk, beaten well

4 1/2 cups sifted powdered sugar
2 teaspoons real vanilla extract

Combine butter and cocoa; cream well. Add remaining ingredients, and beat until smooth.

Spread Coconut-Pecan Filling between the layers and on top of the cooled cake. Spread Mocha Frosting on sides of cake only. If any frosting is left over, cover, and freeze. Great for cupcakes or cookies.

OUR 4TH OF JULY PICNIC

Every year the town of Clifton celebrates the 4th of July with a parade, picnic and fireworks. The quaint Victorian town is so picturesque at this time with the flags and banners flying, and it's a good old-fashioned fun day for the town's residents. This is our family's favorite picnic menu.

Suzi's Fried Chicken

Bayou Burgers

Great Hamburger Buns

Classic Potato Salad

Barbeque Beans

Country Corn Relish

Wanda's Garlic Pickles

Red, White and Blue Salad

Watermelon Fruit Basket

Peppermint Stick Ice Cream

Easy Ice Cream Cookies

Old Fashioned Lemonade

Iced Tea

Suzi's Fried Chicken, see page 200.

Bayou Burgers

Serves 8

2 pounds ground beef
2 eggs, beaten
3/4 cup catsup
2 tablespoons Worcestershire
2 tablespoons finely chopped
  onion
2 teaspoons salt

1/2 cup Victor's blackening
  mix (see page 51)
8 hamburger buns
8 lettuce leaves
8 slices onion
8 slices tomato

Combine first 6 ingredients; mix well. Shape into 8 patties; roll in Victor's blackening mix. Grill patties over medium coals 8 to 10 minutes on each side or until desired degree of doneness.

Place patties on bottom of buns. Top each with lettuce leaf, onion, and tomato slices, cover with bun tops.

Creole or dijon mustard are great on buns.

Great Hamburger Buns

Makes 2 dozen buns

6 cups unsifted flour
2 tablespoons yeast
1 1/3 cups lukewarm water
1 tablespoon sugar

3/4 tablespoon coarse salt
3 tablespoons corn oil
3 large eggs, beaten
sesame seeds

Preheat the oven to 400 degrees.

Sift flour into large mixing bowl. In 2/3 cup of the warm water, sprinkle the yeast and mix well. Pour into flour. Combine sugar, salt, oil and water in a large glass measuring cup. Place in a saucepan filled with warm water over low heat. When mixture is lukewarm, add eggs, reserving 1 tablespoon of egg for brushing on top of buns. Stir until smooth, but not too hot. Now add egg mixture to flour and yeast in bowl and stir into a soft ball. Knead dough in mixing bowl. Oil the surface, cover the dough with a towel, and let rise for about 1 hour. Punch down and knead gently for a few minutes. Roll out dough in 1/4 inch thickness and cut with 3 1/2 inch biscuit cutter. Place rounds on buttered cookie sheet 3 to 4 inches apart. Cover and let rise until nearly doubled in bulk. Brush tops with remaining egg and sesame seeds. Bake at 400 degrees for 20 - 25 minutes.

Barbequed Beans

Serves 6 to 8

3 tablespoons catsup
1 tablespoon prepared
   mustard
2 tablespoons brown sugar
   or molasses

1 teaspoon minced onion
1 can (1 pound) baked beans
3 to 4 strips bacon
1/2 to 1 teaspoon liquid
   hickory smoke

Preheat oven to 350 degrees. Combine catsup, mustard, sugar, onion and liquid hickory smoke; mix this with beans. Place in 1 1/2 quart casserole. Place 3 to 4 strips bacon over top of casserole and bake 25 to 30 minutes.

Wanda's Garlic Pickles

Makes 1 gallon

Cucumbers—Pickling or
   non-waxed cucumbers,
   enough to fill 1 gallon jar
1 quart vinegar, apple cider
1 pint water
1 1/2 cups sugar
1/2 cup coarse salt

3 tablespoons hot pepper
   flakes or 3 large hot red
   peppers
8 garlic cloves
4 tablespoons white mustard
   seeds

Split cucumbers in lengths, remove excess seeds, put in ice water and let stand 3 hours. Combine rest of ingredients, boil until sugar and salt dissolves. Place pickles in gallon jar or crock, pour hot liquid over cucumbers. Let sit several days until flavor develops.

Can be processed in boiling water bath following safe canning procedures.

Classic Potato Salad, see page 200·

Country Corn Relish, see page 91.

Old Fashioned Lemonade, see page 202 .

Ice Tea, see page 202 .

Red, White and Blue Salad

What could be more patriotic?

Serves 6-8

2 cups fresh bluberries
2 3-ounce packages black
  cherry jello
1 8 1/2 ounce can crushed
  pineapple

3 cups boiling water
1/4 cup Maraschino cherries,
  halved

Dressing

1 cup miniature marshmallows
2 cups sour cream

1 teaspoon mayonnaise
1/2 teaspoon real vanilla

Garnish

6 to 8 whole Maraschino
cherries

mint leaves

Dissolve jello in boiling water. Cool. Add pineapple and chill until thickened. Fold in cherries and blueberries. Chill until firm. Mix dressing ingredients and refrigerate several hours or overnight. When ready to serve, stir dressing well and spoon over blueberry mixture.

Watermelon Fruit Basket

Always so festive and colorful for any buffet and everyone appreciates good fresh fruit.

Serves 12

1 large watermelon	2 cups strawberries
(16 to 18 pounds)	2 tablespoons creme de
2 cups honeydew balls	menthe, white
2 cups cantaloupe balls	Fresh mint leaves

Cut watermelon in half crosswise. Cut a thin slice from the bottom of one watermelon half, so that it will sit flat, being careful not to cut through melon. (Save remaining half of watermelon for other uses.)

Draw 1-inch notches around cut edge of top of watermelon. Cut out notches using a sharp knife, and discard.

Scoop watermelon into balls to yield about 8 cups, leaving a 1/2-inch margin of fruit around rim to form shell; remove seeds.

Combine watermelon balls, remaining fruit balls, strawberries and creme de menthe; toss lightly to distribute evenly. Spoon fruit into watermelon shell. Garnish with mint leaves.

Peppermint Stick Ice Cream

I always buy lots of candy canes at Christmas time to use through the year to make this "yummie" ice cream.

Makes 2 quarts

Custard Ice Cream Base

4 egg yolks	2 cups cream (heavy
3/4 cups sugar	whipping cream)
1 cup milk	2 cups half and half

Combine all ingredients, whisk over medium heat until thickened. DO NOT BOIL. Add additional fruit or flavorings. Chill before freezing in ice cream maker.

Peppermint Stick

1 1/2 cups crushed peppermint stick candy (divided)

Add 3/4 cup crushed candy to hot custard mixture, let dissolve in hot mixture, chill; add 3/4 cup crushed candy to chilled mixture before freezing.

Coffee Liqueur

Heat 1/4 cup coffee liqueur with 2 tablespoons instant coffee powder, add to custard.

Vanilla

Add 2 tablespoons REAL vanilla

Fruit

Substitute 2 cups any pureed fruit for 1 cup of the milk and one cup of the half and half. Add 2 tablespoons liqueur to flavor fruit.

Chocolate Chip

Add 1 (6-ounce) package mini-chocolate chips or mint chocolate chips

Let your food processor puree, chop or blend your ingredients. Delicious homemade ice cream can be made in minutes!

Easy Ice Cream Cookies, see page 82.

Old Fashioned Lemonade, see page 202.

Iced Tea, see page 202.

July 4th

Pumpkin Patch

HALLOWEEN APPLE-BOBBING PARTY

There's nothing more fun for adults and children than a great costume party. Halloween is the perfect excuse for us all. This menu should satisfy all ages.

Witches Brew

Jack O'Lantern Cheese

Broomsticks

Deviled Ham Sandwiches

Old Fashioned Pimento Cheese Spread

Autumn Pumpkin Bread

Dried Apple Cake

Goblin Ginger Gems

Hot Toasted Pecans

Harvest Moon Popcorn

Haystacks

Witches Brew

Yield: about 2 quarts

2 quarts apple cider
  (good quality, fresh pressed
  if possible)
1/4 cup lemon juice
2/3 cup firmly packed brown
  sugar

1/2 teaspoon ground allspice
1/2 teaspoon ground nutmeg
1/4 teaspoon salt
12 whole cloves
2 (3-inch) sticks cinnamon

Combine first 6 ingredients in a Dutch oven. Cook over medium-high heat, stirring occasionally to dissolve sugar.

Place cloves and cinnamon on cheesecloth. Bring edges of cheesecloth together at top and tie securely to form a small bag. Drop spice bag into simmering cider mixture; continue to simmer 10 minutes, stirring occasionally. Remove spice bag, pour cider into a heat-proof punch bowl.

Bourbon, rum or applejack can be used to fortify the brew.

Jack O'Lantern Cheese

Yield: 4 cups

1 pound Cheddar cheese,
  grated
8 ounces cream cheese

3 tablespoons brandy
1/2 cup chopped pecans
1/2 cup butter

Combine all in food processor and shape cheese into a pumpkin. Decorate with celery stalk for stem, black olives for face. Place on cheese board and surround with fall leaves. Serve with crackers.

Double to make a large pumpkin.

Broomsticks

Yield: 24

8 stalks washed celery cut into 3-inch pieces

Fill stalks with Old Fashioned Pimento Cheese Spread, cut into 3 inch pieces.

Old Fashioned Pimento Cheese Spread

1 pound grated Cheddar
  cheese
2 4-ounce jars pimento,
  drained

1 cup mayonnaise
dash tabasco
dash worcestershire

Put all the ingredients in a food processor or blender and process until smooth. Spoon mixture onto celery pieces. Remaining spread can be used for sandwiches, put on crackers or used on vegetables.

Deviled Ham Sandwiches

Yield: 3 cups

1 pound cooked ham
  (or leftover cooked country
  ham)
4 tablespoons prepared
  mustard

1/2 cup mayonnaise
1/2 teaspoon Worcestershire
Dash horseradish
Dash tabasco

Chop ham in food processor. Add other ingredients and mix well. Make finger sandwiches or serve with crackers.

Autumn Pumpkin Bread

A moist, spicy bread.

Yield: 2 loaves

2 eggs
1/2 cup vegetable oil
1/3 cup water
3/4 teaspoon salt
3/4 teaspoon ground
  cinnamon
1/2 teaspoon vanilla extract
1 1/2 cups firmly packed light
  brown sugar

1 cup cooked mashed
  pumpkin
1 1/2 cups all-purpose flour
1 teaspoon soda
1/2 cup chopped walnuts
  or pecans
1/2 cup raisins

Preheat oven to 350 degrees. Combine eggs, oil, and water in a large mixing bowl. Add salt, cinnamon, vanilla, and sugar; beat well on low speed of electric mixer. Add pumpkin, mixing well. Mix flour with soda; stir into batter. Fold in nuts and raisins. Pour into 2 greased 1-pound coffee cans or 2 greased 8 1/2 x 4 1/2 x 3-inch loafpans. Bake 1 hour or until loaves test done. Cool in pans on wire racks. Serve with Gingered Cream Cheese. Also good toasted with butter.

Gingered Cream Cheese

8 ounce carton whipped
  cream cheese
2 tablespoons finely chopped
  candied ginger

1 tablespoon orange
  marmalade

Combine all above ingredients.

Dried Apple Cake

A truly Southern, old fashioned cake, delightful with the buttermilk sauce.

Yield: 1 10-inch tube pan

2 cups sugar
1 cup butter
2 1/2 cups dried apples
4 eggs, beaten
1 cup nuts, chopped
4 cups flour

1 box raisins
3 teaspoons soda
1 teaspoon cinnamon
1 teaspoon cloves
1 teaspoon allspice

Preheat the oven to 275 degrees. Cook apples in orange juice to cover. When soft, mash; add sugar and butter to warm apples. Add beaten eggs. Sift flour, soda and spices, add raisins and nuts to sifted flour mixture, stir well. Add floured nut mixture to rest of ingredients, stir well. Spoon batter evenly into brown paper lined and greased 10-inch tube pan. Bake 2 1/2 to 3 hours at 250 to 275 degrees. Remove from pan immediately and cool. Keep cake tightly covered till ready to serve. At serving, cake can be served with warm sauce.

Place a shallow pan of water in the bottom of oven during baking, remove for the last hour. This makes a moister cake.

Buttermilk Sauce

1 cup buttermilk
2 cups sugar

1/2 stick butter
1 teaspoon baking soda

Add soda to buttermilk; add rest of ingredients. Boil down to desired thickness.

Haystacks

Makes 30

1 6-ounce package
  butterscotch chips
1 6 1/2 ounce can peanuts

1 5-ounce can chow mein
  noodles

Melt butterscotch chips in top of double boiler (or microwave). Reduce heat to low; stir in noodles and peanuts until well coated. Remove from heat. Drop by teaspoonfuls onto a sheet of waxed paper. Let cool. Peel from paper and store in airtight container.

Goblin Ginger Gems

This recipe was given to me by my friend, Bette Faries, a wonderful cook, a prize-winning quilter, nurse and textbook author.

Yield: 3 dozen

3/4 cup shortening	2 teaspoons baking soda
1 cup sugar	1/2 teaspoon cinnamon
4 tablespoons molasses	1/2 teaspoon cloves
1 egg	1/2 teaspoon ginger
2 cups flour	1/2 teaspoon allspice

Preheat oven to 325 degrees. Cream first 4 ingredients together until fluffy. Sift remaining ingredients together and add to sugar mixture. Mix well. Chill 1 hour.

Roll into small balls. Roll balls in sugar. Place 2 inches apart on ungreased cookie sheet. Bake about 10 minutes.

Watch closely until edges turn light brown but while the centers are still soft. Very easy to overbake! Cookies will be very brittle.

Hot Toasted Pecans

Yield: 4 cups

1/4 cup butter	1/2 teaspoon hot pepper sauce
4 teaspoons Worcestershire	4 cups pecan halves
1 tablespoon garlic salt	

Preheat the oven to 375 degrees. Melt butter in heavy skillet. Add remaining ingredients. Stir and mix well. Spread out on large flat pan and toast in oven for 30 minutes. Stir while toasting.

These are great to have on hand for unexpected guests.

Harvest Moon Popcorn

Yield: 6 quarts

8 quarts popped popcorn	1 tablespoon ground chili powder
1 1/2 cups melted butter	
1 tablespoon hot pepper sauce	

Melt butter, add seasonings; toss with popcorn.

THANKSGIVING DINNER

Relish Tray

Virginia Peanut Soup

Traditional Roast Turkey

Cornbread Dressing

Giblet Gravy

Whipped White Potatoes

Fresh Buttered Broccoli

Orange Cranberry Relish

Holiday Sweet Potatoes

Mildred's Southern Rolls (Parkerhouse style)

Mother's Apple Pie

Classic Pecan Pie

Bourbon Pumpkin Pie

Praline Mincemeat Cheesecake

Relish Tray

crisp carrot sticks	black and green olives
celery sticks	homemade pickles or relish

Use a beautiful dish to make an attractive assortment of your best pickles and relishes, along with the carrots, celery and olives to whet the appetite and liven up your meal.

Virginia Peanut Soup, see page 118.

Traditional Roast Turkey

Serves 12 to 16

1 (10 to 12 pounds) turkey	1/4 cup butter, melted
2 teaspoons poultry seasoning	1 apple
2 teaspoons salt	1 onion
2 teaspoons pepper	juice of lemon and the rind

Preheat oven to 325 degrees. Remove giblets and neck from turkey, reserve for Giblet Gravy. Rinse turkey thoroughly with cold water; pat dry. Combine salt and pepper; sprinkle over surface and in cavity of turkey. Put apple, onion, lemon juice and rind into cavity, it adds additional flavor.

Close cavity of turkey with skewers. Tie ends of legs to tail with string or tuck them under flap of skin around tail. Lift wingtips up and over back, tucking under bird securely.

Brush entire bird with melted butter; place turkey, breast side up, on a rack in roasting pan. Insert meat thermometer in breast or meaty part of thigh, making sure thermometer does not touch bone. Bake for 4 1/2 to 5 hours, or until the meat thermometer registers 185 degrees. DO NOT OVERCOOK.

Baste turkey frequently with pan drippings. Turkey is done when drumsticks are easy to move.

Transfer turkey to serving platter. Let stand 15 to 20 minutes before carving.

Corn Bread Dressing

Half of our family eats this uncooked and the other half eats it cooked, so we do both.
Serves 12

1/2 cup diced celery
1 cup onion, chopped
2 tablespoons butter
8 cups cornbread crumbs
2 cups white bread cubes
salt to taste
1 teaspoon pepper (or more if
   freshly cracked)

1 tablespoon dried sage, or
   more to taste
4 eggs, beaten
2 cups warm chicken broth,
   or more

Preheat oven to 400 degrees. In a small skillet, saute the celery and onion in the butter until tender. Combine this mixture with all remaining ingredients in a large bowl, and mix together gently but thoroughly. (Make a "wet" dressing, not dry.)

Turn the dressing into a greased 1 1/2 quart round casserole. Bake for 30 minutes.

Giblet Gravy

Makes about 5 cups

giblets (gizzard and heart)
water
6 tablespoons butter
1/2 cup flour

4 cups chicken broth
salt, to taste
2 hard-cooked eggs, diced

Place the giblets in a saucepan and add enough water to cover. Bring the water to a boil and simmer, partially covered, until the giblets are tender, about 1 hour. Drain and finely chop (you will have to remove the rubbery outer membrane of the gizzard).

In a saucepan, melt the butter. Stir in the flour. Add the broth and cook, stirring constantly, until the mixture thickens and comes to a boil. Season with salt and stir in the giblets and eggs.

Liver and neck can be used along with the giblets, if desired.

Whipped White Potatoes, see page 120.

Fresh Buttered Broccoli

Serves 8 to 10

3 pounds fresh broccoli   3 tablespoons melted butter

Wash broccoli. Peel tough stems, break off florets. Cut stems into diagonal 1/2 inch pieces.

Cook in 1/2 to 1 cup water until crisp and tender. DO NOT OVERCOOK. Drizzle melted butter over broccoli, serve.

Orange Cranberry Relish

1 12-ounce package   1 apple
  cranberries   1/2 cup sugar
1 orange

Wash, cut up and remove seeds from orange. Wash core and remove seeds from apple and cut in quarters; put along with cranberries and sugar into food processor and grind. Best made a few days ahead to set flavors. Can also add Triple Sec, or any other orange-flavored liqueur.

Holiday Sweet Potatoes

Southerners love sweet potatoes. This is a good recipe for any family gathering.
Serves 8 to 10

4 1/2 cups mashed sweet   2 eggs, beaten
  potatoes, cooked   1/4 cup Grand Marnier
1/2 cup butter, melted   1/4 cup orange liqueur (good
1 20-ounce can crushed   quality)
  pineapple, including juice   2 tablespoons grated orange
3/4 cup light brown sugar   rind
1 5.33 ounce can evaporated   1 cup miniature
  milk   marshmallows
1/2 cup raisins   1/2 cup chopped pecans.

Preheat oven to 350 degrees. Puree sweet potatoes and butter in food processor. Combine with pineapple and juice, sugar, milk, raisins, and eggs. Mix well. Add Grand Marnier, orange liqueur, and orange rind. Pour into buttered casserole. Sprinkle marshmallows and pecans on top. Bake 20 minutes.

Mildred's Southern Rolls, see page 209.

Mother's Apple Pie

My mother gave me this pie filling recipe. We always had wonderful cooking apples in our yard and she used to "put up" apples in the freezer. Just make the filling, freeze, and thaw anytime you need to make an apple pie.

Makes 1 (9-inch) pie

Pastry for 2-crust 9-inch pie
3 or 4 ample cups peeled,
   sliced thin apples
1 stick butter
2/3 cup orange juice

pinch of salt
1 cup sugar
4 tablespoons flour
1/2 teaspoon cinnamon
1/2 teaspoon cloves

Preheat oven to 450 degrees. Combine apples, butter, orange juice and a pinch of salt. Put on stove, bring to boil, stirring. Mix sugar, flour, cinnamon and cloves; add to boiling mixture, cook 1 minute. Cool; put mixture into unbaked pie shell and cover with top crust. Bake for 15 minutes. Reduce heat to 350 degrees and bake 30 to 40 minutes longer.

Perfect Piecrust

Makes 2 (9-inch) double crust pies and 1 pie shell

4 cups unsifted all-purpose
   flour, lightly spooned
   into cup
1 tablespoon sugar
2 teaspoons salt
1 3/4 cups solid vegetable
   shortening, not refrigerated,
   DO NOT use oil, lard,
   margarine or butter

1 tablespoon white or cider
   vinegar
1 large egg
1/2 cup water

Combine first 3 ingredients in large bowl and mix well with table fork. Add shortening and mix with fork until ingredients are crumbly.

In small bowl, beat together with fork 1/2 cup water, vinegar and egg.

Combine the two mixtures, stirring with fork until all ingredients are moistened. Divide dough in 5 portions, shape in flat round patty; wrap in plastic, chill 1/2 hour. The portions may be put in freezer. Thaw before using.

One tablespoon of flour rubbed into a baked or unbaked pastry shell before adding filling will help prevent sogginess.

Classic Pecan Pie, see page 178.

Bourbon Pumpkin Pie

Kentucky, Tennessee, and Virginia boast of good bourbons. Choose your favorite to flavor this pie.

Makes 1 (9-inch) pie

2 tablespoons butter
3/4 cup sugar
3 eggs
1/2 teaspoon salt
1/4 teaspoon ginger
1/4 teaspoon nutmeg

1/2 teaspoon cinnamon
1 cup canned pumpkin
1 cup evaporated milk
1/4 cup bourbon whisky
1 (9-inch) unbaked pastry
   shell

Preheat oven to 450 degrees. Cream butter and sugar. Beat in eggs, one at a time, by hand or with electric mixer. Add remaining ingredients, beating after each addition. When well blended, pour into pastry shell and bake for 10 minutes. Reduce heat to 325 degrees and continue baking for about 45 minutes or until custard is firm.

For a different taste any winter squash can be substituted for pumpkin.

Praline Mincemeat Cheesecake

Ann Simpson, a Clifton friend, gave me this delicious cheesecake recipe. It is absolutely scrumptious!

Makes 1 (9-inch) pie

1/2 cup butter
1 cup graham cracker crumbs
1/4 cup sugar
2 8-ounce packages cream
cheese, softened
1 (14-ounce) can sweetened
condensed milk
1 envelope unflavored gelatin
(2 1/2 teaspoons)

1/4 cup lemon juice
1 1/3 cups mincemeat
1/2 cup chopped pecans
1 tablespoon grated lemon
rind
1 cup whipping cream,
whipped

In saucepan, melt butter; stir in crumbs and sugar. Pat firmly on bottom of 9-inch springform; chill.

In large mixer bowl, beat cheese until fluffy. Add sweetened condensed milk, beating until smooth.

In small saucepan, soften gelatin in lemon juice, heat and stir until dissolved. Add to cheese mixture with mincemeat, nuts and rind, mix well. Thoroughly fold in whipped cream; turn into prepared pan. Chill 3 hours or until set. Garnish with dollop of whipped cream—drizzle with praline liqueur.

To make ahead: Line sides of springform pan with wax paper; proceed as directed but do not garnish. Wrap entire pan tightly, freeze. Thaw in refrigerator. Remove sides of pan before serving. Garnish.

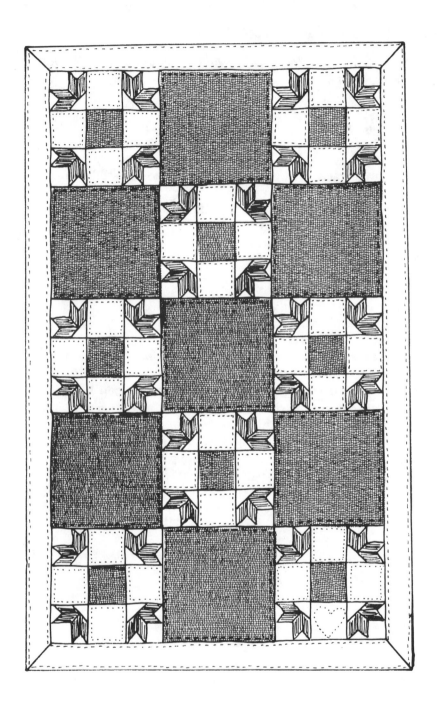

Turkey Tracks

CHRISTMAS EVE DINNER

Hot Holiday Tea Punch
Old Fashioned Scalloped Oysters
Christmas Eve Beef Carbonade
French Bread with Herb Butter
Marinated Cauliflower and Broccoli Salad
Ambrosia

The memories of Christmas time with my grandparents, Mama & Pop Norrod, includes their country store in Hanging Limb, Tennessee. It was a wonderland with barrels of nuts in their shells, citrus fruits from Florida, candy containers loaded with Christmas cane candy, candied orange slices, gum drops, hard Christmas candy mixture, and chocolate covered cherries. My grandmother, like my mother, would bake many cakes, pies, and candies for several weeks of holiday entertaining. I was fascinated by my grandmother's larder, stocked with really old old fashioned canned meats and fruits. I loved looking out her hand crocheted covered windows at the snow falling while she worked on her Christmas baking. My handsome, blue eyed, white haired French grandfather would spoil me with many treats from the store while I sat on his knee to hear him sing "A frog he would a courting go", or "She'll be coming around the mountain".

My father and I would always chop down our own Christmas tree and I would get to bake cookies, or string popcorn or cranberries for decoration. Some years we would make snow soap (it was great fun, but what a mess later.)

We would always share Christmas with my sister Dianne, her husband Nick, and her son GeeBee. Between the good food and a visit from Santa Claus- what more did a child need? My oldest sister Wanda, with her 5 children would visit sometime during the holiday season and we would prepare Christmas dinner all over again!

I hope you can use some of our holiday recipes for your family and that they become memories and tradition for you too!

159

Hot Holiday Tea Punch

Cheers!

Makes 1 gallon

2 cups water
5 tea bags

3 sticks cinnamon
14 cloves

Into boiling water, add teabags, cinnamon and cloves. Steep 15 minutes.

1 large package cherry jello
1/2 cup sugar

2 cups boiling water

Mix above ingredients. Combine with first mixture.

1 12-ounce orange juice
concentrate
1 12-ounce frozen lemonade
concentrate

1 #2 can pineapple juice

Combine above juices and add to rest of mixture, adding enough water to make 1 gallon.

Serve hot or cold. Lasts for weeks and is a cherry holiday color.

Old Fashioned Scalloped Oysters

We make this for Travis. He loves oysters in any shape, form or fashion!
Serves 8

1 quart oysters with liquor
1 1/2 cups heavy cream
1 cup dry bread crumbs
1 1/2 cups cracker crumbs

1 cup melted butter
salt
paprika

Preheat oven to 400 degrees. Drain the oysters and combine the liquor with the cream. Mix the bread crumbs and cracker crumbs and pour the butter over them. Plan to use 2 layers of oysters and 3 layers of crumbs. Grease a baking dish and cover it with a layer of crumbs; then proceed to build up the other alternating layers of oysters and crumbs, seasoning each layer of oysters with salt and paprika; pour 1/2 of the liquor and cream mixture over each oyster layer. The top layer of crumbs should be dry; dot it with butter. Bake the casserole for 20 minutes.

Christmas Eve Beef Carbonade

This is a wonderful stew to make ahead, freeze, and reheat when needed, especially for a busy holiday season.

Serves 8

4 pounds boneless chuck cut
   in 2x4 inch strips
1/4 cup salad oil
4 large onions, thinly sliced
1 tablespoon brown sugar
4 cloves garlic, minced
1 cup beef stock
1/2 teaspoon thyme
pinch of nutmeg

1 bay leaf
1 teaspoon salt
2 tablespoons dijon mustard
2 tablespoons wine vinegar
2 to 3 cups beer
5 slices French bread,
   crumbed
3 tablespoons chopped parsley
1 1/2 pounds fresh mushrooms

Preheat oven to 325 degrees. In a large heavy casserole, heat half of the oil, and brown meat a few pieces at a time. Set meat aside. In same casserole, saute onions and mushrooms until tender, adding oil as needed. Sprinkle brown sugar over the onions and cook stirring for a minute. Return meat to casserole and add garlic, stock, thyme, nutmeg, bay leaf, salt, vinegar, mustard and parsley, with enough beer to cover meat. Place bread crumbs on top of meat mixture. Cover casserole and place on lower rack of oven. Cook for 2 hours or until tender. Liquid will be reduced to about half.

French Bread with Herb Butter, see page 31.

Marinated Cauliflower and Broccoli Salad

The colors of Christmas, red, green, and white!

Serves 10 to 12

1 head cauliflower	1 2-ounce jar chopped
2 bunches broccoli	pimento, drained

Wash and drain vegetables. Break cauliflower and broccoli tops into small flowerets. Slice broccoli stalks very thin (peel if stalks are tough). Pour Lemon Herb Dressing over vegetables, cover and marinate overnight.

Lemon Herb Marinade or Salad Dressing

Makes 3 1/2 cups

2 cups good quality olive oil	3 tablespoons thyme
1 cup fresh lemon juice	3 tablespoons grated lemon
1 cup chopped parsley	peel
5 small garlic cloves, minced	2 tablespoons salt
5 tablespoons sugar	1 teaspoon pepper (cracked)

Combine all ingredients, blend thoroughly. Chill.

Ambrosia

Ambrosia is a truly Southern Christmas tradition.

Serves 10 to 12

15 to 18 medium-size oranges	1 can (13 1/2-ounce)
3/4 cup sugar	pineapple chunks
1 1/2 cups fresh coconut, coarsely grated	

Peel oranges, being careful to remove all white membrane. Cut into small slices or pieces. Mix oranges and juice with sugar. Add coconut and pineapple chunks. Place in refrigerator to chill.

1/4 to 1/2 cup good quality liqueur can be drizzled over to "dress up" for dessert.

CHRISTMAS BRUNCH

Fresh Fruit Cup
Country Ham and Eggs
Cheesy Garlic Grits
Christmas Red Cinnamon Apples
Geba's Famous Biscuits
Wonderful Winningham Waffles
Brown Sugar Syrup
Red Raspberry Jam – Strawberry Preserves
Daddy Shorty's Coffee

Fresh Fruit Cup

Use Ambrosia from Christmas Eve Dinner. Add a sprinkling of chopped dates to the mixture and add a red maraschino cherry and a green spearmint gumdrop leaf for decoration on individual servings.

Country Ham with Red-eye Gravy

Slice Country Ham 1/3 inch thick. Score fat edges to keep ham from curling. Place ham in iron or heavy skillet and cook slowly, turn, cook until fat is transparent.

Remove ham, keep warm; add 1/2 cup strong coffee to pan drippings in skillet, 1/2 tablespoon brown sugar and bring to a boil. Reduce down. Serve over ham and biscuits.

Eggs

Break one egg per person into heavy, hot skillet that is gilded with shortening or fat, add tablespoon or so of water, cover with lid, cook just a few minutes for easy up, few more minutes for medium up and still more minutes for hard up.

Garlic Cheese Grits

If you haven't tried grits, try these!

Serves 4 to 6

4 cups water
1 clove garlic, finely minced
1/2 teaspoon salt
1/8 teaspoon pepper
1 cup quick-cooking grits

2 tablespoons butter
1 1/4 cups shredded Cheddar
  cheese, divided
2 eggs, beaten
1/2 cup milk

Preheat oven to 350. In large saucepan, bring the water to a boil, adding the garlic, salt, and pepper. Gradually stir in the grits. Lower the heat and simmer, stirring occasionally, 5 minutes.

Remove the pan from the heat and stir in the butter and 1 cup Cheddar cheese until the butter melts. Mix the eggs with the milk and stir thoroughly into the grits.

Turn the grits into a greased 2-quart round casserole. Sprinkle with the remaining 1/4 cup cheese. Bake for 1 hour, or until set and browned.

Grits are also delicious made with chopped fresh herbs. Add several spoonfuls in your favorite grits recipe or add to garlic cheese grits.

Christmas Red Cinnamon Apples

My uncle and aunt, Mr. and Mrs. William T. Norrod, of Cheyenne, Wyoming, took us on a delightful picnic to Fort Laramie. Aunt Janie's mother, Mrs. John Wespe, made several of the dishes that day. Our Sarah was enthralled by her. Mrs. Wespe invited Sarah and our family to tea so Sarah could see her extensive doll collection. She was very gracious in giving me several of her favorite recipes. We've really enjoyed this colorful, holiday or anytime dish.

Serves 6 to 8

3 cups sugar
1 1/2 cups water
2/3 cups red cinnamon
   candies

1/2 teaspoon red food
   coloring
6 medium size tart apples,
   cored and sliced into rings

Combine first four ingredients in large sauce pan, bring to a boil, stirring until sugar and candies are dissolved.

Add apples to syrup and simmer covered until apples are tender; about 10 minutes, turn frequently. Remove from heat and allow to stand about 20 minutes or until apples are evenly colored.

Wonderful Winningham Waffles

Winningham's have a sweet tooth. My father loves these. Our family always uses Hickory Bark Syrup from a family recipe. It's very difficult to make and you need to be near shaggy bark hickory trees to make it. As a quick substitute, we often made this brown sugar syrup.

2 cups flour, measured after
   sifting
1/2 teaspoon salt
2 tablespoons sugar
3 rounded teaspoons baking
   powder

2 eggs, separated
1 1/2 cups, milk
3/4 cups melted fat (half
   vegetable shortening, half
   butter)

Sift flour with salt, sugar, and baking powder. Beat the yolks with the milk and pour slowly into the dry ingredients, stirring to prevent lumping. Add melted fat and beat until batter is smooth, then fold in the two well-beaten whites.

Bake on waffle iron according to instructions for machine.

Brown Sugar Syrup

Makes 5 cups

4 cups sugar	2 cups water
1/2 cup firmly packed brown	1 teaspoon maple extract
sugar	1 teaspoon vanilla extract

Combine sugars and water in saucepan. Bring to a boil. Boil very slowly for 15 to 20 minutes. Remove from heat; cool slightly. Stir in maple and vanilla extracts. Let stand until completely cool. Pour into covered container. Refrigerate.

Strawberry Jam

2 10-ounce packages frozen,	1 package powdered fruit
sweetened strawberries	pectin
3 cups sugar	1 cup water

Thaw frozen berries and grind or blend in blender to make a puree. Add sugar, mix thoroughly and let stand 20 minutes, stirring occasionally.

Combine powdered pectin and water and boil rapidly for 1 minute, stirring constantly.

Remove from heat, add the fruit to the pectin; stir for 2 minutes. Pour into clean containers; cover with tight-fitting lids. Let stand at room temperature 24 hours. If jam does not set, refrigerate until it does. Freeze or refrigerate.

Red Raspberry Jam

3 10-ounce packages of	4 cups sugar
frozen raspberries	1/2 cup liquid pectin

Thaw frozen berries and grind or blend in blender to make a puree. Add sugar, mix thoroughly and let stand 20 minutes, stirring occasionally. Add fruit mixture to pectin, mix thoroughly.

Pour into clean containers; cover with tight-fitting lids. Let stand at room temperature 24 hours. If jam does not set, refrigerate until it does. Freeze or refrigerate.

This jam requires no cooking.

Strawberry Preserves

This is a true old recipe for preserves. It is delicious. Our daughter Sherry eats all the jars we can put up!

1 quart strawberries   **3 cups sugar**

Mix berries and 1 1/2 cups sugar. Boil 5 minutes. Sift remaining sugar *slowly* into the fruit mixture so as not to stop boiling. Boil 10 to 15 minutes longer or until berries are transparent. Skim if any froth collects on surface. Pour into earthen jar or in crockery bowl. Let stand 24 hours, stir occasionally, pour into hot sterilized jars and seal with paraffin, or put into clean crock or jar in refrigerator or may be frozen.

Important – cook in small quantities, one quart at a time.

Daddy Shorty's Coffee

My father has always been known for his delicious coffee. We think the secret is his drip coffee maker which has survived 53 years of marriage. The pot has been thrown away several times, and is always returned. It still makes wonderful coffee every day, and Daddy Shorty's reputation is still intact!

Geba's Famous Biscuits, see page 59.

Christmas Tree

CHRISTMAS DAY DINNER

Yuletide Oysters
Crown Roast of Pork with Pepper Jelly Glaze
Cornbread Dressing
Creamed Brussel Sprouts and Onions
Whipped Turnips
Holiday Sweet Potatoes
Norwegian Cranberry Sauce
Rosy Red Watermelon Rind Pickles
Geba's Spoon Rolls
Christmas Desserts

Yuletide Oysters

This is a very festive way to start your meal.

Serves 6

24 oysters
1/3 cup finely chopped green
pepper

1/3 cup finely chopped red
pepper or pimento

Vinaigrette:

1/4 cup wine vinegar
1/2 cup good quality olive oil
salt

freshly cracked pepper
hot pepper sauce to taste

Preheat oven to 450 degrees. Place oysters on cookie sheet. Sprinkle chopped peppers on top of unbaked oysters. Drizzle vinaigrette over tops. Bake in hot oven until edges curl (DO NOT OVERCOOK) about 5 minutes, or run under broiler.

Serve oysters on salad plate covered with a doily, surround with lots of green parsley, cherry tomatoes and lemon wedges.

Crown Roast Of Pork

A crown roast is spectacular. You'll receive "ooh's and ahh's" when this is presented at the table.

Serves 8

1 crown roast of pork, made from two center cut pork loins made into a crown roast with bones Frenched, and roast tied ready for roasting. (Order ahead from the butcher.)
1 cup red pepper jelly
1/2 cup apple juice or cider
cherry tomatoes, for garnish

parsley or watercress, for
garnish

Preheat oven to 350 degrees. Cover the bone ends of the crown roast with foil and place a wad of aluminum foil in the center of the roast to help keep its shape. Place in a shallow pan, not on a rack, and roast about 20 minutes to the pound or until the internal temperature is 160 degrees.

Glaze with melted pepper jelly and juice or cider, the last 15 minutes of baking.

When ready to serve, remove the string from the roast, place on a platter, fill the center with Cornbread Dressing (see page 153). Put cherry tomato on bone ends and place parsley or watercress around edges to make a wreath. Remaining pepper jelly glaze can be passed around to be used on roast.

Pepper Jelly

Easy to make, colorful, and a taste treat.

Makes 3 pints

1/4 cup finely chopped red or
    green hot peppers
1 1/2 cups finely chopped
    sweet green peppers
6 1/2 cups sugar

1 1/2 cups vinegar
1 bottle liquid pectin
green or red food coloring
    (optional)

Mix peppers, sugar, and vinegar. Bring to a boil; boil 3 minutes. Stir in pectin, boil 1 minute more. Remove from heat; let stand 5 minutes. Add food coloring if desired. Pour into hot sterile jars and seal.

Delicious with cold meats, sandwiches, and cream cheese on crackers.

Creamed Brussel Sprouts and Onions

Serves 8

2 10-ounce tubs brussel
    sprouts
1 pound small white
    onions
2 tablespoons butter
2 tablespoons flour

1 cup milk
nutmeg to taste
salt and pepper to
    taste

Wash sprouts, trim and peel onions. Let stand in cool, salted water. Boil vegetables until tender, drain. Heat butter in saucepan, add flour, cook for a few minutes over medium heat, gradually add milk, whisking constantly until thickened, add vegetables, and seasonings to taste.

Whipped Turnips

Try these turnips, so good!

Serves 8 - 10

3 pounds turnips, peeled and
    sliced
1/2 cup butter

1/4 to 1/2 cup heavy cream
salt and pepper

In a medium saucepan boil turnips in water to cover. Cook until tender. Drain. Whip with mixer, add butter, cream, salt and pepper until light and fluffy.

Rosy Red Watermelon Rind Pickles

Very old-fashioned, and helps you use up the whole watermelon.

Makes 8 to 10 pints

1 very large, firm watermelon	12 cups sugar
1 cup salt	4 sticks cinnamon
4 cups cider vinegar	2 tablespoons whole cloves
2 cups strained red cherry juice (from fresh, cooked or canned cherries)	

Remove rind from watermelon. Peel off outside skin, then cut rind into 3-inch strips (there should be 12 cups of cut-up rind). Place strips in a large jar. Cover with water to which 1 cup salt has been added. Let stand overnight.

The next morning, drain off all water. Place rind and 2 quarts fresh water in a large saucepan, Boil for 10 minutes. Drain.

In a 6-quart kettle bring vinegar, cherry juice and sugar to a boil. Add spices, tied loosely in a cheesecloth bag, and simmer 10 minutes. Remove spices. Drop cooked melon strips into hot syrup. Cook until syrup thickens and is transparent.

Put a cinnamon stick and 3 whole cloves into each hot jar, then fill with boiling hot preserves. Adjust lids. Process in boiling water bath (212 degrees) for 15 minutes. Remove jars and let cool.

Holiday Sweet Potatoes, see page 154.

Norwegian Cranberries Sauce

Makes 2 cups

1 16 ounce package FRESH cranberries	2 cups sugar

Take an electric mixer. Beat cranberries with sugar. Do this repeatedly every 30 minutes for 1 day until sugar is dissolved. Keeps indefinitely in refrigerator.

Geba's Spoon Rolls, see page 128.

Christmas Desserts, see page 173.

CHRISTMAS DESSERTS

Christmas Coconut Cake
Granny Crawford's Fruit Cake
Family Fruitcake
Tennessee Jam Cake
Classic Pecan Pie
Geba's Iron Skillet Chocolate Pie
Orange Slice Cookies
Candied Orange Peel
Sherry's Favorite Fudge
Bourbon Balls
Toffee Butter Crunch
Spiced Walnuts
Old Fashioned Christmas Custard
Tennessee Tom and Jerry

Thoughts of wonderful holiday foods evoke nostalgic feelings and hopes that traditions continue after I'm gone. The Christmas recipes that follow are tried and true traditional Southern desserts.

Christmas Coconut Cake

There is nothing more spectacular or showy for holiday entertaining than this coconut cake. To our family, it wouldn't be Christmas without one.

20 to 24 servings

1 cup butter or margarine
  (or white shortening)
2 cups sugar
3 1/4 cups sifted cake flour
2 teaspoons baking powder
pinch of salt

1 cup milk
2 teaspoons real vanilla
8 egg whites
Seven Minute Boiled Frosting
1 coconut

Preheat oven to 375 degrees. Cream butter; gradually add sugar, beating until light and fluffy.

Combine dry ingredients. Add flour mixture to creamed mixture alternately with milk, begin and end with flour mixture. Add vanilla.

Beat egg whites (room temperature) until stiff peaks form. Fold into batter. Pour batter into three greased and floured 9-inch round cake pans. Bake for 20 minutes or until a broom straw or wooden pick comes out clean.

Cool for 10 minutes in pans, invert on cake rack and cool completely.

Sprinkle coconut liquid on layers and frost with Seven Minute Boiled Frosting. Frost each layer, top and sides.

Seven Minute Boiled Frosting

2 egg whites
1 1/2 cup sugar
1/3 cup water

1/4 teaspoon cream of tartar
pinch of salt
1 teaspoon vanilla

Combine egg whites, water, cream of tartar and salt, place over double boiler. Beat with electric mixer about seven minutes or until frosting holds shape. Add vanilla.

Coconut

Pierce the three eyes of the coconut with an ice pick and drain the liquid (save to sprinkle on cake). Bake the coconut in a 400-degree oven for 15 minutes. Split the coconut in half and loosen the coconut meat from the shell. Remove the brown membrane with vegetable peeler or small sharp knife. Cut the coconut into pieces and grate in food processor or hand grater.

Cover the layers, tops, and sides with the freshly grated coconut.

This cake will freeze beautifully. Freeze uncovered until hard. Insert wooden picks on top to hold plastic film off of cake cover with plastic wrap, then cover with a good covering of heavy duty foil.

Granny Crawford's Fruit Cake

Granny Crawford lived across the street as a child. She wasn't my granny, but a dear neighbor. She left several good recipes with our family.

Makes 2 cakes

1 (14-ounce) package
  shredded coconut
2 (8-ounce) packages dates,
  chopped
1/2 pound candied cherries,
  chopped

1/2 pound candied pineapple,
  chopped
2 cups english walnuts,
  chopped
2 cups pecans, chopped
2 cans condensed milk

Preheat oven to 300 degrees.

Combine first 6 ingredients, then add milk. Gently fold all together and put into 2 papered and greased 8 1/2 x4 1/2 x 2 1/2 pans, bake at 300 degrees for 1 hour. DO NOT OVERBAKE. Let cool for 1 hour in pan. Remove, cool on cake rack.

Family Fruitcake

Fruity, dark, and Very Rich!!
Makes 4 to 5 9x5-inch loaf pans

Can be made months before Christmas. Sprinkle with good quality rum and wrap in cheesecloth in tightly closed container. Store in cool dark place.

2 pounds cherries, candied	1/2 teaspoon salt
2 pounds pineapple, candied	1 teaspoon soda
1/2 pound citron	1 1/2 teaspoons cinnamon
1/2 pound oranges, candied	2 teaspoons cloves, powdered
2 pounds currants	3 1/2 teaspoons allspice
2 pounds white raisins	1 cup molasses (dark black)
1/2 pound lemon, candied	1 1/2 cups flour
1 cup rum for soaking fruit	2 pounds pecans, chopped
1 pound butter	1 dozen eggs, beaten
1 pound dark brown sugar	4 1/2 cups flour
1 cup boiling water	1 cup wine or rum

Soak fruit for 2 days in 1 cup rum (more if desired, keep adding). Stir occasionally and cover.

Preheat oven to 250 degrees. Line greased pans with brown paper and grease again over the paper. Cream butter and sugar. Pour 1 cup boiling water over salt, soda and spices. Add molasses and stir. Sift 1 1/2 cups flour over fruit and nuts and toss lightly. This keeps fruit and nuts from sinking to bottom. Add beaten eggs to butter and sugar mixture. Add flour, wine, spices and fruit which has soaked for 2 days and then tossed with flour. Pour mixture in the pans. Bake at 250 for several hours until small crack forms in center and a toothpick inserted into crack comes out clean. Remove from pans immediately. Cool on cake rack.

Tennessee Jam Cake

Bijou Looper Watkins, a cousin from Chattanooga, Tennessee, gave mother this cake recipe many years ago. It not only makes a delicious devil's food cake, but with the addition of jam makes a memorable jam cake.

Bijou's Devil Food Cake - to make Jam Cake

1/2 cup water	2/3 cup shortening
1 1/2 teaspoon soda	1 3/4 cups sugar
1/2 cup cocoa	2 eggs
2 1/2 cups flour, all purpose	1/2 teaspoon salt
3/4 cup sour milk (1 teaspoon lemon juice added to 3/4 cup milk)	1 teaspoon vanilla
	1 heaping cup blackberry jam

Preheat oven to 250 degrees.

Combine first 3 ingredients and allow to stand while mixing rest of cake. Cream shortening and sugar until fluffy. Add eggs, one at a time, beating well after each addition. Add vanilla. Combine salt and flour. Add flour and milk alternately to creamed mixture, beginning and ending with flour.

Stir in first 3 ingredient mixture. Add 1 heaping cup of jam. Pour batter into 3 well greased and floured 9-inch round cake pans. Bake at 250 degrees for 1 hour. Cool in pans 10 minutes; remove from pans and cool completely.

Spread Fruit Icing between the layers and on top of cooled cake. Spread Creamy Mocha Icing on sides of cake.

Fruit Icing

2 cups sugar	1 cup figs, ground
1 1/2 cups milk	1 cup raisins, ground
1 cup nuts, ground	

Boil sugar and milk, add nuts, figs and raisins, bring to a boil, then cool.

Creamy Mocha Icing, see page 136.

Classic Pecan Pie

Serves 8

3 eggs
1 cup sugar
3 tablespoons flour
1 cup dark corn syrup
1 cup chopped pecan pieces

3 tablespoons melted butter
1 tablespoon real vanilla
1 9" unbaked deep dish pie
  shell

Preheat oven to 400 degrees. Beat eggs thoroughly, add sugar, flour and syrup. Next add pecans, butter, then vanilla. Pour into unbaked pastry shell.

Bake at 400 degrees for 10 minutes, lower heat to 350. Bake approximately 30 more minutes. (DO NOT OVERBAKE.)

Serve with sweetened whipped cream, so rich . . .

Geba's Iron Skillet Chocolate Pie

This is my mother's Geneva Winningham of Cookeville, Tennessee, Chocolate Pie recipe. As a child this was our everyday favorite pie. Now at the restaurant it is the number one dessert sold!

Serves 6 Chocoholics or 8 smaller servings

2 cups sugar (see note)
1/2 cup butter or margarine
5 eggs separated
2 1/4 cups milk
4 rounded tablespoons dry
  cocoa

4 rounded tablespoons flour
1 teaspoon real vanilla
1 9" pie shell (deep dish)

Mix all dry ingredients. Melt butter or margarine in 10" iron skillet (or Teflon lined skillet). Add dry mixture, mix lightly. Combine beaten egg yolks with milk, add to mixture, stirring constantly. Cook slowly until really thick. Remove from heat, add vanilla, blend well and pour into baked pie shell.

Cool and serve with sweetened whip cream.

The sugar mixture can be cut by 1/3 to 1/2 if you desire a less sweet chocolate.

Also you can make a meringue of the 5 egg whites (room temperature) to which a pinch of salt, pinch of cream of tartar and 1/4 teaspoon vinegar have been added. Beat until stiff and add 10 tablespoons of sugar until well blended. Put on pie, pile high with uneven finish. Bake at 350 degrees for 10 to 12 minutes.

Orange Slice Cookies

Growing up, I spent many hours at Harvey and Ova McCulley's house with their daughter Sara. Ova made these chewy holiday cookies and I was always fascinated with her putting candy in a recipe.

Makes 54 bars

1 pound orange slice candy	2 cups sifted flour
1/2 teaspoon salt	1 pound brown sugar
4 eggs, slightly beaten	1 cup chopped nuts
1 teaspoon real vanilla	

Cut candy into small pieces. Add remaining ingredients and mix well. Spread in 2 greased 9x9x2-inch pans. Bake at 350 for about 45 minutes. Cut in 1x3-inch bars and roll in powdered sugar.

Candied Orange Peel

Yield: 1/2 pound

2 large oranges (thick)	1 cup water
2 cups sugar	2 tablespoons light corn syrup

Cut peel of each orange into quarter sections, pull away from pulp. Cut quarters into 1/8" inch strips. Place in saucepan, cover with cold water and bring to a boil. Simmer 10 to 15 minutes or until tender. Drain, combine sugar, water, syrup in saucepan. Stir over low heat until sugar is dissolved. Add orange peel and cook 25 to 30 minutes until peel is clear and syrup is thick. Remove peel from syrup, drain. Roll strips in granulated sugar.

Keep orange peel on hand to decorate desserts and add zing to many sauces.

Sherry's Favorite Fudge

Geba makes this every Christmas for all of us. However, she learned to make a separate batch for Sherry or we would never eat any.

Yield: 5 pounds

5 cups sugar
1/2 pound butter
1 large can evaporated milk
1 8-ounce jar marshmallow
cream

1 12-ounce package chocolate
chips
2 cups nut meats
2 teaspoons real vanilla

Butter a 9x13-inch pan. Mix sugar, milk and butter, bring to a boil. continue stirring constantly for 10 minutes. Remove from heat and add rest of ingredients. Mix until smooth and pour into buttered pans. Cut into desired size.

Bourbon Balls

These are delicious with an after dinner coffee.

Yield: 3 dozen

1 small box vanilla wafers
1 cup chopped pecans
1 cup powdered sugar
2 tablespoons cocoa

1 1/2 tablespoons white corn
syrup
2 jiggers bourbon whiskey

Roll vanilla wafers into fine crumbs. Mix the crumbs with sugar, cocoa and nuts. Dissolve corn syrup in whiskey and add to dry ingredients. Mix well to blend. Mixture must be moist enough to hold together. Form into small balls and roll in additional powdered sugar.

Toffee Butter Crunch

Yield: Makes 1 small tin.

1 1/4 cups butter
1 2/3 cups sugar
4 teaspoons corn syrup
1/4 cup water
1 1/2 teaspoons instant coffee powder

1 teaspoon salt
1/2 cup coarse chopped nuts
1/2 pound milk chocolate, chopped
1 cup finely chopped nuts

Mix first 7 ingredients together in heavy saucepan and cook to 300 degrees. Pour onto oiled cookie sheet, sprinkle chopped milk chocolate on top of hot mixture and spread as it melts and top with nuts. Break into pieces.

Spiced Walnuts

Just one of those added "extras" that makes your entertaining special.

Yield: 2 1/2 cups

2 1/2 cups walnuts
1 cup sugar
1/2 cup water

1 teaspoon cinnamon
1/2 teaspoon salt
1 teaspoon vanilla

Toast 2 1/2 cups walnuts in 375-degree oven for 5 minutes; stir once. In buttered saucepan combine sugar, water, cinnamon and salt. Bring mixture to a boil stirring until sugar dissolves. Cook to soft ball stage without stirring. Remove from heat; add vanilla and beat for 1 minute or until mixture is creamy. Add nuts and stir gently until nuts are well coated. Pour mixture onto buttered cookie sheet, separate with fork.

Old Fashioned Christmas Custard

This is the Tennessee version of eggnog, it's thinner in texture but is very rich in taste! We traditionally always serve this with Christmas Coconut Cake.

Serves 12

6 beaten egg yolks
2 tablespoons cornstarch
5 cups scalded milk
1 cup milk to add to beaten
   yolks

3/4 cup sugar
1 tablespoon real vanilla
   (teaspoon or more to taste)

Scald milk (heat milk until small bubbles form and a "skim" usually forms), remove "skim", add eggs, milk mixture, sugar mixed with cornstarch and whisk thoroughly.

Cook over double boiler, or heavy saucepan until custard coats a metal spoon. Be careful to cook slowly so that the eggs don't curdle, whisk constantly, add vanilla and chill.

Serve with a dusting of freshly grated nutmeg. (Rum or Bourbon may be added to taste).

Tennessee Tom and Jerry

This is a wonderful drink for a cold wintry night; not as rich as the Christmas Custard but just as satisfying.

Serves 12

6 eggs, whites and yolks
   beaten separately
12 tablespoons sifted
   powdered sugar
1/2 teaspoon ground allspice

1/2 teaspoon ground cloves
1 teaspoon ground cinnamon
Whiskey (Tennessee)
Jamaica Rum

Fold the yolks and whites together after beating, adding the sifted powdered sugar and spices. Put 2 tablespoons of this mixture in the bottom of a Tom and Jerry Mug or a regular coffee cup. Add a jigger of whiskey, warmed in the bottle but not heated. Then stir well to make an emulsion. This keeps the mixture from curdling. Add 1/2 teaspoon warmed Jamaica rum along with each jigger of whiskey, if the flavor is liked. Fill up the mugs or cups with boiling water, stirring as the water is poured. Serve at once, as the spices have a tendency to settle at the bottom of the mug.

WEDDING RECEPTION

We cater many weddings at the Heart in Hand as well as off the premises. We have catered for 10 people to 500 people, as formal as you can get, to dinner on the lawn. This menu is our favorite wedding menu. It can be adapted for many other special occasions.

Baked Tennessee Country Ham

Geba's Famous Biscuits

Rosemary Sliced Beef

Orange-Nut Muffins

Smoked Turkey Breast

Parkerhouse Rolls

Hot Crab and Artichoke Dip

Crackers

Baked Brie with Almonds

Crusty French Bread

Herb Stuffed Mushrooms

Crudites

Curried Honey Dip

Fresh Herb Dip

Bleu Cheese dip

Spiced Walnuts

Salmon Mousse

Watermelon Fruit Basket

Celebration Champagne Punch

Wedding Punch

Wedding Cake

Baked Tennessee Country Ham, see page 101.

Geba's Famous Biscuits, see page 59.

Rosemary Roast Beef

The aroma of the herbs and beef cooking whets the appetite.

Serves 25 - 30

12 pound roast beef (well trimmed, boneless, top quality round)	freshly cracked pepper
	garlic powder
	bacon strips (if needed)
Rosemary	

Preheat oven to 325 degrees. Place roast, fat side up on rack in roasting pan. Cover liberally with crushed rosemary, pepper and garlic powder. Secure bacon strips on top if there is no layer of fat to baste meat while cooking. Cook approximately 2 1/2 hours for medium rare or until meat thermometer registers 140 to 150 degrees. Let stand at least 15 minutes before carving. May be chilled after cooking and sliced very thin.

Orange Nut Muffins, see page 13.

Smoked Turkey Breast

Thin, smoked slices are so elegant and delicious.

Serves 24

1 (8-pound) turkey breast	1/4 cup pepper
1/4 cup vegetable oil	1 cup vinegar
1/2 cup salt	

Prepare charcoal fire in smoker and let burn 10 to 15 minutes. Place water pan in smoker and fill with vinegar. Add enough hot water to fill pan, if necessary.

Place turkey breast on food rack. Cover with smoker lid; cook about 16 hours, refilling water pan with water if needed.

Transfer turkey to a serving platter. Let stand at least 15 minutes before slicing.

A whole turkey may also be used

Depending on the intensity of the heat in your smoker, less hours may be needed to cook the turkey breast.

Parkerhouse Rolls, see page 121.

Hot Crab and Artichoke Dip

This is the most asked for dish when we cater. My friend Donna Keummerle craves this stuff. This is for you, Donna!

1 1/2 pounds lump crabmeat	1/2 teaspoon white pepper
1 pound cooked artichoke hearts (if canned or frozen, drain thoroughly)	1 teaspoon garlic salt
	1/2 teaspoon cayenne pepper
	1/2 teaspoon paprika
8 ounces cream cheese	1 teaspoon Worcestershire
1/4 cup mayonnaise	2 teaspoons lemon juice
1/4 cup sour cream	few dashes red hot sauce
1 teaspoon Old Bay Seasoning	

Preheat oven to 350 degrees. Process artichokes into food processor until well chopped but not mushy. Place in large bowl with crabmeat. Process all the other ingredients until well mixed. Add to crabmeat and artichokes.

Bake in a 9x13 glass baking pan, foil covered for 25 minutes. Serve with crackers or French bread slices.

Baked Brie with Almonds

Serves 50

1 2.2 pounds wheel of Brie cheese	1/4 cup melted butter
1/2 cup sliced, blanched almonds	

Preheat oven to 350 degrees. Place brie wheel on baking sheet. Top with almonds and butter. Bake approximately 15 minutes to toast almonds and heat the cheese. DO NOT OVERCOOK. Carefully remove, with 2 large spatulas, to attractive serving platter. Surround with black or green grapes, grape leaves or fresh mint and serve with French bread slices.

Herb Stuffed Mushrooms

These disappear quickly!

20 mushrooms

8 ounces cream cheese
1 teaspoon garlic, finely
  chopped
2 tablespoons green onions,
  finely chopped
1 tablespoon chopped
  tarragon, fresh
1 tablespoon chopped basil,
  fresh

1/2 tablespoon chopped
  oregano, fresh
1/2 teaspoon white pepper
1/2 teaspoon garlic salt
1/2 cup finely minced parsley,
  fresh (no substitute)
20 large mushroom caps

Clean and stem mushrooms. Process all other ingredients in food processor until well combined. Mixture should be a light green color. Pipe or spoon into mushroom caps.

Dried herbs may be substituted. Be sure and taste first.

Spiced Walnuts, see page 181.

Salmon Mousse, see page 103.

Watermelon Fruit Basket, see page 141.

Crudites

The items available in the marketplace for a bountiful crudite platter are endless with the year round supply of standard vegetables, as well as the gorgeous new baby vegetables. We display large mounds of each vegetable in an artful arrangement in old baskets, dough trays, or lettuce lined copper trays. It's beautiful on any buffet line or cocktail table. Make sure the vegetables are fresh, thoroughly cleaned, sliced, then beautifully arranged.

Artichokes, tiny
Asparagus, tips or blanched
  stalks
Avocados, fingers dipped in
  lemon juice
Green Beans, tiny
Broccoli buds, raw or
  blanched
Carrots, baby, or blanched
  sticks
Cauliflower, small florets
Celery, strips
Cucumber, strips, seeds
  removed

Mushrooms
Onions, green
Peas, tiny snow peas or sugar
  snap
Peppers, green, yellow, red
  in strips
Radishes, little red, icicle
Tomatoes, cherry, plum,
  yellow or red
Squash, young yellow, or
  zucchini, cut in disks or
  strips
Turnips, young turnips, thinly
  sliced

Edgar's Bleu Cheese Dressing

Edgar Santa-Cruz, one of our kitchen staff members, makes all our salad dressings. This is his recipe for bleu cheese dressing and its GOOD!

Makes 1 quart

3/4 cup mayonnaise
3/4 cup sour cream
1/4 cup chopped green onion
1/2 teaspoon white pepper
1/2 teaspoon cumin

10 dashes tabasco
1/3 cup half and half
1/2 cup buttermilk
2 cups crumbled bleu cheese

Combine all above and refrigerate.

Honey Curry Dip

Unusual but very tasty.

Makes 3 cups

1/2 cup honey	1/2 cup green onion, chopped
1 stick butter	1 1/2 cups mayonnaise
3 tablespoons curry powder (good quality)	

Heat honey, butter and curry powder, until curry is blended. Cool, then add onions and mayonnaise.

Herb Dip

Makes 2 cups

8 ounces cream cheese, room temperature	2 tablespoons chopped green onions
3 tablespoons sour cream	1 tablespoon fresh tarragon
3 tablespoons mayonnaise	1/2 teaspoon dried dill weed
1 teaspoon finely chopped garlic	1/2 teaspoon white pepper
	1 teaspoon garlic salt

Combine all ingredients, blend until smooth.

Celebration Champagne Punch, see page 100.

Wedding Punch

Non alcoholic

Makes 1 gallon

6 cups cranberry juice	1 cup pineapple juice
1 12-ounce can limeade	1/2 cup sugar
3 cups orange juice	5 cups gingerale

Combine first five ingredients, just before serving, add gingerale. Serve in beautiful punch bowl with heart shaped ice ring. Garnish with fresh mint and strawberries.

For heart shaped ice ring, fill heart mold with thinly sliced lemons, limes, and oranges, cover with gingerale and freeze until solid. Unmold right before serving.

DERBY DAY BUFFET

Tennessee Mint Julep
Polo Room Smash
Potted Pork with Sage
Shrimp Paste – Crackers
Country Ham with Biscuits
Chicken Hash on Corn Meal Battercakes
Marinated Artichoke Hearts and Olives
Overnight Walnut-Herb Salad
Black Bottom Pie
Extra Special Brownies
Little Chess Cakes
Lemon Bars

Tennessee Mint Julep

Make a simple syrup by boiling 2 cups of sugar and 2 cups of water for 5 minutes, without stirring. Add 1/2 teaspoon peppermint extract. Fill a jar loosely with sprigs of fresh mint (uncrushed) and cover with the cooled syrup; cover and refrigerate 12 - 24 hours. Discard mint. Make 1 julep at a time.

Fill a chilled julep cup with finely crushed ice, pour in half a tablespoon of the mint flavored syrup and 2 ounces of the very best Tennessee Bourbon. Stick in a sprig of mint and serve at once.

To frost a drink - Grasp rim of the filled julep cup with your fingertips and rapidly twist the cup back and forth until the outside is covered with a heavy frost, or churn with a spoon.

Polo Room Smash

Travis has played polo for many years. Through the years we collected many old polo prints and memorabilia. They were perfect for the decor of one of our dining rooms, thus the Polo Room.

Makes 1 gallon

1 bottle bourbon (quart)	1 (12-ounce) can frozen
1 cup sugar	lemonade concentrate
1 dozen lemons	

Cut lemons in half, squeeze into crock of glass gallon container. As you squeeze each lemon also drop in the shell. Add bourbon, sugar and lemonade and stir until sugar dissolves. cover and refrigerate overnight. Remove lemons before serving. Serve in cups packed solid with finely crushed ice.

Can be made ahead in volume for large gatherings or taken to picnics or tailgate parties.

Country Ham with Biscuits

Baked Tennessee Country Ham, see page 101.

Geba's Famous Biscuits, see page 57.

Place a 2-inch square country ham on each buttered biscuit.

Potted Pork with Sage

As delicious as a pate, without the liver.

Makes 2 pints.

4 pounds pork from the back,
loin, or ribs
3/4 pound salt fatback,
trimmed rind and well
rinsed
7 cloves garlic, chopped

2 teaspoons marjoram
2 - 3 teaspoons sage
2 teaspoons thyme
salt and freshly ground black
pepper
tabasco

Cut the pork into 3-inch strips and the fatback into small cubes. Place the fatback in a large pan. Cook over low heat until it renders some fat. Add the pork and enough water to cover the meat, about 1 cup. Partly cover the pan and cook over low heat for 45 minutes, without browning, stirring from time to time. Check to be sure there is enough water in the pan to prevent the pork from drying out and browning. When done, the meat should be white and tender. Remove, saving the liquid and fat, and with 2 forks pull the meat into shreds. Place in a bowl, taste for seasoning, and add most of the liquid and fat to moisten. Taste again and adjust seasonings. Place in crock or jar, wrap tightly and refrigerate or freeze.

To store indefinitely, put clarified butter on top of crock or jar to seal.

Shrimp Paste

A delicious old Kentucky recipe.

Makes about 2 cups

1 1/2 pounds cleaned shrimp,
cooked
1/2 green pepper
1/2 Bermuda onion
2 tablespoons Vinegar

1 1/2 tablespoons Worcestershire
1 tablespoon dry mustard
salt and pepper
tabasco
1 stick butter, softened

Chop finely in food processor the green pepper and onion. Pour off the juice and drain in a colander. Chop the shrimp. Combine, add seasonings and mix well. Mash in the butter with a fork, working it until thoroughly blended. Pack in a mold and chill. Unmold and garnish with parsley. Serve with crackers.

Chicken Hash

Serves 12

1 1/2 quarts cooked chicken,
  diced
1/4 cup butter
3 medium onions, finely
  chopped
1/2 bunch celery, finely sliced
3 medium potatoes, finely
  chopped

1 quart rich chicken stock
ground pepper to taste
1/2 teaspoon chicken bouillon
  granules
1/3 cup browned flour

Saute the onions in butter until browned. Add them with the potatoes and celery to the stock. Cover and cook until potatoes are done. Taste for seasoning. Mix flour with an equal amount of cold water and thicken the stock. Cook for 10 minutes. Add the chicken and simmer gently. It may be cooled, refrigerated and reheated slowly without letting it boil.

How to brown flour

Brown 2 - 3 cups of flour at a time in the oven. Spread it out in a baking pan and place it in a 350-degree oven for 25 to 30 minutes, stirring with a fork so that it will brown evenly. Store in a jar.

To make turkey hash, substitute turkey for the chicken.

This also makes an excellent luncheon entree with a cranberry side dish.

Corn Meal Battercakes

Makes 16 to 18

1 cup buttermilk
1/2 teaspoon baking soda
1 egg, beaten slightly
2/3 cup white cornmeal

3/4 teaspoon salt
3 tablespoons melted bacon
  fat or butter
1/4 cup water

Stir soda into buttermilk and add to egg. Stir in other ingredients. Drop by heaping tablespoons on hot griddle. Turn over when browned and bubbles form. Cook until done.

Marinated Artichoke and Olive Salad

Good make-ahead dish as well as a good keeper.

Serves 6

1 lb. fresh mushrooms
1/4 cup chopped pimentos
4 12-ounce can artichoke
  hearts, drained
1/2 cup chopped green onions
1/2 cup stuffed olives,
  drained and sliced

1 large can pitted black
  olives (whole)
6 cloves garlic
Lemon Herb Salad Dressing

Wash, and trim and quarter mushrooms. Drop into boiling salted water and boil for 1 minute. Drain and put in bowl. Quarter artichokes and add to mushrooms. Add onions, olives and garlic. Make Lemon Herb Dressing (page 162) and pour over vegetables. Refrigerate overnight. Stir several times. Serve on crisp lettuce lined bowl.

Overnight Walnut-Herb Salad

1 cup walnuts, divided
1 teaspoon salad oil
1/4 teaspoon garlic salt
1/8 teaspoon dill weed
4 cups finely shredded lettuce
or mixed greens
6 - 8 cherry tomatoes, halved

1 cup shredded Cheddar
cheese
1 10-ounce package frozen
green peas, cooked and
cooled or
1 16-ounce can tiny peas
Creamy Dressing

Place walnuts in rapidly boiling water; boil 3 minutes, drain well. Toss with oil, garlic salt, and dill. Place on shallow baking sheet; toast at 350 degrees for 10 minutes, stirring once; cool. Layer ingredients in large glass bowl in following order: 2 cups lettuce or greens, cherry tomatoes (cut sides against glass), cheese, peas, 3/4 cup walnuts and remaining greens. Top with 1 cup Creamy Dressing; seal to edges of bowl. Cover; chill several hours or overnight. Before serving sprinkle with remaining walnuts.

Creamy Dressing

Makes 1 1/2 cups

3/4 cup mayonnaise
1/2 cup sour cream
2 tablespoons chopped green
onion

1 tablespoon lemon juice
2 teaspoons chopped parsley
1 teaspoon prepared mustard
1/2 teaspoon salt

Combine all ingredients; blend well.

Black Bottom Pie

Yield: 1 (9-inch) pie

1 envelope unflavored gelatin
1 3/4 cups milk, divided
1 cup sugar, divided
1/2 teaspoon salt
4 teaspoons cornstarch
4 eggs, separated
1 1/2 ounces unsweetened
  chocolate, melted

1 teaspoon real vanilla
1 (9-inch) gingersnap crust
2 tablespoons rum or bourbon
1 cup whipping cream
2 tablespoons powder sugar
1/2 cup chopped pecans
Shaved chocolate

Soften gelatin in 1/4 cup milk. Scald remaining milk in double boiler. Mix 1/2 cup sugar, salt and cornstarch. Add egg yolks, beat until thick and lemon colored. Slowly add to hot milk, stirring constantly. Cook, stirring constantly, until custard is thick and coats metal spoon. Remove from heat; strain, if necessary, to remove any lumps. Remove 5 tablespoons custard; set aside. Add softened gelatin to remaining custard; stir until gelatin is dissolved. Chill until mixture begins to thicken. Stir together chocolate, reserved custard, and vanilla. Beat with rotary beater. When cool, spread chocolate mixture over crust. Beat egg whites until soft peaks form; gradually add remaining sugar, continuing to beat until stiff, but not dry. Fold rum and beaten egg whites into chilled custard. Pour over chocolate layer in pie shell, chill until firm. Whip cream with powdered sugar. Spread over pie. Sprinkle with pecans and shaved chocolate. Refrigerate until ready to serve.

Gingersnap Crust

14 gingersnaps, crushed
  (whirl in food processor)

5 tablespoons melted butter

Preheat oven to 350 degrees. Combine gingersnap crumbs and butter. Pat mixture along the bottom and sides of a nine-inch pie pan. Bake 8 to 10 minutes. Cool.

A graham cracker or chocolate wafer crust can be substituted for the gingersnap crust.

Really Good Brownies

These are wonderful for any occasion!
Makes 4 to 5 dozen

4 squares unsweetened
  chocolate
1 cup butter
2 cups sugar
4 eggs

1 cup flour
1/2 teaspoon salt
1 teaspoon vanilla
1 cup chopped nuts

Preheat oven to 325 degrees. Melt chocolate and butter together. Add sugar. Beat eggs lightly and add to mixture. Add flour, vanilla nuts and salt. Bake for 30 to 35 minutes in a 9x13-inch pan.

Frosting

3 cups powdered sugar
4 tablespoons butter
1/4 teaspoon peppermint
  extract

Heavy cream
Drops of green food coloring

Icing

4 squares semisweet chocolate

2 tablespoons butter

Melt chocolate with butter

Combine powdered sugar and butter. Add enough cream to make mixture a spreading consistency. When brownies are cool, spread with frosting. When frosting is set, ice brownies. Add peppermint extract and coloring if mint frosting is desired.

Little Chess Cakes

As a child at Capshaw Elementary School, I would swap food at lunch for these! We had terrific Southern cooks at school who made homemade breads and desserts each day. These taste like Little Chess Pies.

Makes 4 dozen

3/4 cup butter	2 1/4 cups dark brown sugar
1 1/2 cups sifted flour	3 egg yolks
3 teaspoons granulated sugar	1 cup pecans, chopped
1/2 teaspoon vanilla	3 egg whites

Cream butter. Add slowly the sifted flour and granulated sugar. Pat into a 9 x 13 inch pan with 1 1/2-inch sides. Bake 20 to 30 minutes in a 375 degree oven, or cook until the crust is golden brown. Meanwhile, make the filling by mixing the dark brown sugar with the beaten egg yolks. When thick and spongy add the pecans. Add vanilla and fold in the stiffly beaten whites. Spread filling evenly over the crust. Return pan to oven and cook 25 to 30 minutes longer, or until the filling sets. Do not cook too long, as the filling should be transparent and semi-soft, never hard or chewy. Dust with powdered sugar and when cool, cut into squares.

Lemon Bars

Makes 32 bars

1/2 cup butter	1/2 teaspoon baking powder
1/4 cup powdered sugar	1/4 teaspoon salt
1 cup flour	2 tablespoons flour
2 eggs, beaten	3 tablespoons lemon juice
1 cup sugar	lemon rind

Preheat oven to 350 degrees. Cream first 3 ingredients and press in a 9-inch square pan. Bake 15 minutes at 350 degrees. Add together the beaten eggs, the sugar, baking powder, salt and flour. Then add the lemon juice and lemon rind. Pour over a crust and return to a 350-degree oven for 25 minutes. When cool, dust with powdered sugar.

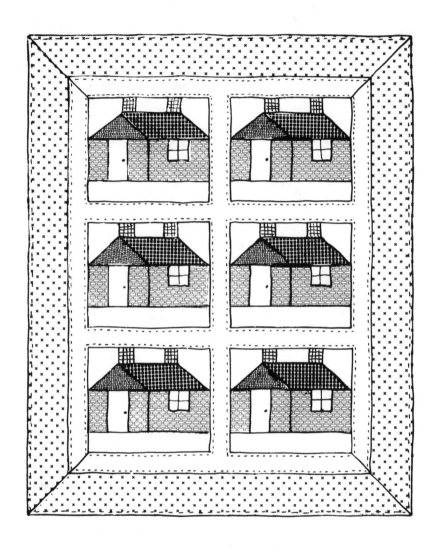

Schoolhouse

CLIFTON ELEMENTARY SCHOOL
6TH GRADE BANQUET

When our daughter Sherry "graduated" from sixth grade, we catered the school dinner. We let the sixth graders pick the menu.

Suzi's Fried Chicken

Classic Potato Salad

Garden Salad with Tomato French Dressing

Mildred's Southern Rolls

Really Good Brownies

Old Fashioned Lemonade

Iced Tea

Suzi's Fried Chicken

I've been making this chicken since the age of eight. I still "love" this the best!

Serves 12

3 (2 1/2 to 3-pound) broiler
   fryers, cut up
3 cups all-purpose flour
1 1/2 teaspoons salt
1 teaspoon black pepper

1 teaspoon paprika
1/2 teaspoon garlic powder
1/2 teaspoon poultry seasoning
3 cups buttermilk
Vegetable oil

Preheat the oven to 375 degrees. Combine flour and seasonings in roomy pan. Pour buttermilk into another pan. Place each piece of chicken in flour mixture, shake excess flour off, dip in buttermilk, then re-dip in flour mixture, coating well. Repeat with all pieces of chicken.

Heat 1 inch of oil in large heavy skillet to 350 degrees; add several pieces of chicken to hot oil and fry until golden brown on each side; only turn one time! As chicken browns, lay on baking sheet and finish cooking in oven until done. Drain chicken well on paper towels.

To test oil, drop a 1-inch cube of bread into oil. If it's browned in 1 minute, the oil is the right temperature. Too high, the chicken will burn; too low, the chicken will be soggy. Depending on the chicken piece, cooking time varies from 20 to 35 minutes.

Classic Potato Salad

Serves 12

12 medium size new potatoes
4 hard-boiled eggs
1 1/2 cups finely diced celery
2 onions finely diced
1/2 cup chopped sweet
   pickles
3 tablespoons sweet pickle
   juice

1 1/2 cups salad dressing
1 teaspoon salt
1/2 teaspoon freshly ground
   black pepper
2 dashes hot pepper sauce
1 tablespoon prepared
   mustard

Cook potatoes in boiling water until tender (not mushy). Drain well and cool. Peel and cut into 1/2 inch dice.

Combine all ingredients except one hard-boiled egg; slice one for garnish. Finely chop the other eggs. Toss to coat well. Put into an attractive lettuce lined bowl. Garnish with the one sliced egg, pimento strips, olives or sliced sweet pickles.

Garden Salad with Tomato Dressing

This tomato dressing is a childhood favorite of mine and is good on any lettuce. Keeps well in the refrigerator.

Serves 12-15

2 medium heads of iceberg
lettuce, bite-size pieces
1 small head red cabbage,
finely sliced
1 head green leaf lettuce,
bite-size pieces
10 green onions, sliced on
diagonal
2 carrots, coarsely grated

1 pint cherry tomatoes,
halved
3 cucumbers, peeled and
thinly sliced
3 green peppers, cut into thin
strips
1 bunch radishes, thinly
sliced

Prepare all vegetables. (Everything but lettuce can be done in food processor.) Toss in large salad bowl. Pass dressing separately for a crowd so that salad won't get soggy.

Tomato Dressing

Makes 1 quart

1 can tomato soup
(condensed)
3/4 cup apple cider vinegar
1 1/2 cups vegetable oil
1 tablespoon paprika
1 teaspoon salt
1/2 teaspoon freshly ground
pepper

1 tablespoon Worcestershire
2 cloves garlic, minced finely
1 small onion, minced finely
1/3 cup brown sugar, firmly
packed

Shake together well or prepare in food processor. Chill. Shake before serving.

Mildred's Southern Rolls, see page 209.

Really Good Brownies

Makes 18 large brownies

1 1/3 cups all purpose flour	4 eggs
1 teaspoon baking powder	1/4 cup milk
1/2 teaspoon salt	1 tablespoon real vanilla
1 cup unsalted butter	extract
1 cup cocoa	1 cup chopped pecans
2 cups sugar	

Preheat the oven to 350 degrees. Spray a 9 x 13 x 2-inch baking pan with vegetable spray. Set aside. In a small bowl, combine flour, baking powder, salt. Set aside. In a medium saucepan (or microwave) melt butter. Add cocoa and stir to blend. Pour into large bowl. Add sugar and blend with electric mixer. Add eggs, blend. Add flour mixture, beat until smooth. Add milk and vanilla, blend. Stir in pecans. Pour into prepared pan. Bake for 25 minutes. Brownies are done when a toothpick inserted into center comes out clean. DO NOT OVERBAKE! Let cool. Cut into 2 x 3-inch pieces.

Old Fashioned Lemonade

This is a true lemonade and it tastes so...good!

Serves 10

2 cups sugar	1 1/2 cups freshly squeezed
1/2 gallon water (total)	lemon juice

Put 2 cups sugar and 2 cups of the water in saucepan to boil until sugar dissolves. Cool. Add lemon juice and rest of water. Chill. Serve over lots of ice with a sprig of fresh mint and a thin slice of lemon.

Iced Tea

All of us from the South seem to live on iced tea. This is a fool-proof version.

Makes 1 gallon

10 good quality tea bags	3 cups cold water

Bring the 3 cups cold water to boil in a stainless steel saucepan. Drop in teabags. Turn off heat immediately. Cover. Let steep until cool. Remove bags which have been gently squeezed to remove all liquid (do not break teabag). Add enough cold water to make a gallon. Garnish with orange, lemon or lime slice and fresh mint sprig.

If a sweet version is called for, add 1/2 to 1 cup sugar to boiling water before adding teabags.

"DOWN BY THE RIVER" FAMILY REUNION

Amen!

My Mother's family, "the Specks" and "the Norrods" always congregate Memorial Weekend "down by the river", at the old family cemetery and land in Tennessee. It's a beautiful spot where everyone enjoys visiting and eating delicious food as well as respectfully paying tribute to their ancestors.

Celebration Baked Ham

Jezebel Sauce

Suzi's Barbequed Fried Chicken

Sherry Diane's All Purpose Spaghetti Sauce

Sarah's Macaroni and Cheese

Country Cole Slaw for a Crowd

Gooey Good Sweet Potatoes

T'NT Black-eyed Peas

Geba's Pickled Beets and Eggs

Wanda's Garlic Pickles

Mildred's Southern Rolls

Ginny's Favorite Banana Split Cake

Cousin Ann's Wacky Cake

Moma Norrod's Oatmeal Cake

Wanda's Haystack Pie

Aunt Lula's Mudhen Cookies

Old Fashioned Lemonade – Iced Tea

Celebration Baked Ham

In the South, we love ham and no gathering would be complete without it!
Serves 20 to 24

1 quart champagne, ginger ale or cola	1 1/2 cups dark brown sugar
1 quart water	2 tablespoons prepared mustard
1 pint molasses	Whole cloves
1 ham weighing 12 to 20 pounds	1 large can pineapple rings
	Maraschino cherries

Preheat the oven to 325 degrees. Just before baking, weigh the ham. Place it in a large roaster. Pour the molasses, water, and champagne, gingerale or cola over it. Cover the roaster with lid or aluminium foil and bake the ham in a moderate oven, 325 degrees, allowing 15 minutes to each pound. If the liquid evaporates, it will be necessary to add more water from time to time. When ham is tender, remove it from the oven and with a knife trim top skin (do not throw it away, it gives a fine flavor to beans, greens, or cabbage). Dice the ham fat but do not cut through to the meat. Into each little square of fat, place 1 whole clove. Smear the mustard over the surface of the fat. Pat on brown sugar. Anchor pineapple rings with toothpicks, put a maraschino cherry in center of each pineapple. Drizzle 1/2 cup sweet sherry over. Bake for 30 minutes; increase heat 375 to 425 degrees, until ham is beautifully glazed.

Jezebel Sauce

Makes 4 cups

3 ounces horseradish	1 (18-ounce) jar apple jelly
1 (1 3/8 ounce) can dry mustard	1 tablespoon coarsely ground black pepper (more if you prefer really spicy)
1 (18-ounce) jar pineapple preserves	

Blend horseradish and mustard. Add remaining ingredients, stirring until thoroughly blended. Refrigerate, keeps well for months.

Suzi's Barbequed Fried Chicken

This is two favorites rolled into one! Try this for a gathering—everyone will love the chicken.

Serves 12

1 recipe Suzi's Fried Chicken
Chicken Barbeque Sauce
1 cup oil
1 1/2 cups tomato catsup
1 1/2 cups chopped onions
1/2 cup water
2/3 cup lemon juice

6 tablespoons sugar
6 tablespoons Worcestershire
4 tablespoons prepared
  mustard
3 teaspoons salt
1 teaspoon black pepper

Preheat oven to 350 degrees. Cook onions in oil until tender. Add remaining ingredients and cook slowly for approximately 1 hour.

Place chicken which has been fried (UNDERCOOK, BUT BROWN THE CHICKEN BEAUTIFULLY) into a large baking pan. Coat with Barbeque Sauce. Bake 20 to 30 minutes until chicken is done. Yum!

Sherry Diane's All Purpose Spaghetti Sauce

My older sister Diane was a wonderful cook. She introduced me to lamb, veal, and many ethnic dishes. Every Christmas she would bake over 20 different kinds of cookies for the holidays. She always encouraged me to do well in anything I attempted and was always on hand with encouragement. She and her only son were killed in a tragic car accident. This is one of the first recipes that she sent Mother when she first got married.

"Mother, for spaghetti for about 4 to 5 persons, I use your dutch oven. I cover the bottom of pan with oil. I chop an onion up and 1 to 1/2 (depends on size) cloves of garlic. I let that brown, then add 1 can tomato paste and cook that in oil and onion mixture for a few minutes. Then I add 1 can tomato puree (the size of a soup can) and then add water. (You know how much water.) Then I add about 2 big tablespoons of parsley, dash of allspice, sugar (white), salt, and pepper. Cook for a couple of hours.

Use whatever meat you want. You brown your meat separately then add it to the tomato sauce. Something that is delicious is to get stewing veal, cut up into small pieces, then brown and cook in sauce. Also, when using veal either throw in a couple of pork chops or ribs. Ribs are delicious. If you make meat balls, use about 1/2 clove of garlic, plenty of breadcrumbs, egg, salt and pepper, and parsley. Don't put onion in then; make the meat balls small, and roll them until they are good and solid.

If you want to make for a bigger bunch, add one more can of tomato sauce. The small size can of tomato sauce—if you can't find tomato puree use 2 small cans in place, and if making for more, add one more can. I hope you understand this."

Love,
Diane

Oil

1 onion

1 1/2 garlic cloves

1 can tomato paste

1 large can tomato puree (or 2 cans small tomato sauce, if you want more for Company add one more can tomato sauce)

water

2 big tablespoons parsley

salt

pepper

sugar (white), about 2 to 3 teaspoons

dash of allspice (good dash)

Sarah's Macaroni and Cheese

Our Sarah loves this dish. In fact she has eaten it so many times, I often thought she would turn into macaroni!!

Serves 6 to 8

1 (8-ounce) package elbow macaroni, cooked	1 egg, slightly beaten
	3/4 teaspoon salt
2 cups cream style cottage cheese	2 cups shredded sharp Cheddar cheese
1 (8-ounce) carton sour cream	paprika

Preheat oven to 350 degrees. Drain and rinse macaroni, set aside. Blend cottage cheese, sour cream, egg, salt, and Cheddar. Fold in macaroni. Spoon into lightly greased 2-quart casserole. Sprinkle with paprika. Bake for 30 minutes or until heated through.

Country Coleslaw for a Crowd

This is a traditional, cooked dressing, favored in the South. The dressing can be used for potato, seafood, ham and fresh vegetable salads.

Serves 24

Shred 4 small heads of green cabbage very, very fine. There should be about 8 cupfuls. Put in a bowl of ice water and let stand 20 minutes. Drain, pat dry in a towel, and mix with a dressing made as follows:

8 well-beaten eggs	4 teaspoons salt, or more to taste
4 tablespoons flour (rounded)	
1 cup apple cider vinegar	8 tablespoons sugar (to taste)
12 tablespoons sweet or sour cream	4 tablespoons butter or olive oil
2 teaspoons dry mustard	1 cup water

To the well-beaten eggs add flour, mustard, salt and sugar. Beat until smooth and creamy. Slowly add water mixed with vinegar. Pour into saucepan, add butter and set over a low flame, stirring constantly. Let cook until thick. The mixture will lump, but do not be discouraged. Remove pan from stove and beat and beat and beat the mixture until smooth once more. Add cream and correct the seasoning. Cool. Mix with the shredded cabbage.

Gooey Good Sweet Potatoes

These are gooey and good!

Serves 6-8

3 cups cooked mashed sweet
  potatoes
1 cup sugar
1/2 cup butter
2 eggs

1 teaspoon real vanilla
1 teaspoon cinnamon
1 teaspoon nutmeg
1/3 cup milk

Preheat oven to 350 degrees. Mix all above ingredients and put into a well buttered oven proof 9 x 12-inch pan. Combine and crumble the following mixture on top and bake for 40 minutes.

1/2 cup butter
1 cup brown sugar

1 cup chopped pecans
1/3 cup flour

T'NT Black-eyed peas

Tennessee and Texas-style peas—unusual and always asked about on a buffet table.

Serves 4-6

2 (10-ounce) packages frozen
  black-eyed peas, cooked and
  drained
1/2 cup olive oil
1/2 cup vegetable oil
1/4 cup white wine vinegar

4 cloves garlic, crushed
1/2 cup thinly sliced green
  onion
1/2 teaspoon salt
cracked black pepper
1 teaspoon red pepper flakes

Combine all ingredients and marinate at least 24 hours.

This can be doubled and is a good keeper in the refrigerator

Excellent served on a bed of lettuce, with tomato slices, red onion rings, and Jalapeno pepper.

Geba's Pickled Beets and Eggs

Daddy always grows the tiniest beets, so wonderful pickled!

Serves 12

24 small beets	6 whole cloves
1 cup cooking liquid	1 (3-inch) stick cinnamon
1 pint vinegar	3 medium onions, sliced
1 1/4 cups sugar	1 dozen hard boiled eggs
2 tablespoons salt	

Remove beet tops, leaving roots and 1-inch stems. Cover with boiling water, cook until tender. Drain, reserving 1 cup cooking liquid. Remove skins. Combine cooking liquid, vinegar, sugar, salt and spices. Heat to boiling point. Add beets and onions. Simmer 5 minutes. Remove from heat. Add hard boiled eggs.

Let sit 24 hours or more for flavor to develop and color eggs.

1 long red hot pepper, 1 (1-inch) slice fresh ginger may be added to hot cooking liquid to make spicier beets and eggs.

To make hard boiled eggs: cover 12 eggs with cold water, add 1 teaspoon salt, bring to hard boil. Cover tightly. Turn off heat. Let set 30 minutes. Drain, let set in cold water 30 minutes. Peel.

Mildred's Southern Rolls

Yield: 6 dozen

1 quart sweet milk	8 cups flour
1 cup sugar	1 teaspoon baking soda
1 cup shortening	1 teaspoon salt
2 packages yeast	1 teaspoon baking powder

Preheat oven to 450 degrees. Heat milk, sugar and shortening until scalded, not boiling. Allow to cool to lukewarm. Dissolve 2 packages yeast in 4 tablespoons lukewarm water in separate cup, then add to ingredients above. Add 4 cups flour (will be soft, even soupy, but this is the secret to good rolls). Set this aside to rise until double in bulk (about 1 hour). Then add soda, salt, baking powder, and 4 more cups of flour or enough to make a dough that can be handled without sticking. Put in refrigerator and use as needed. When ready, roll out, cut and let rise for about 1 1/2 hours. Bake in shallow greased pan for about 10 minutes or until done.

Can be made into tiny party rolls or regular size dinner rolls.

Ginny's Favorite Banana Split Cake

*This recipe was given to me by Helen Crawford, a dear neighbor in my child-
hood. She was a good country cook. Our daughter Ginny always asks for this
cake on her birthday.*

Serves 12

5 bananas	1 #2 can crushed pineapple
3 sticks butter	(well drained)
2 cups graham cracker	2 cups heavy whipping cream,
crumbs	whipped
2 eggs	1 small package pecans
2 cups powered sugar	1 small jar maraschino cherries

Mix one stick butter (melted) with graham cracker crumbs, pat into
13 x 9 x 2-inch pan, bake at 325 degrees for 15 minutes.

With electric mixer, beat 2 eggs, 2 sticks butter, and 2 cups powdered
sugar; spread over cooled crust.

Cover with sliced bananas, spread on crushed pineapple and cover
with whipped cream. Sprinkle with nuts and chopped cherries. Cover and
refrigerate overnight.

Wanda's Garlic Pickles, see page 139.

Aunt Lula's Mudhen Cookies, see page 41.

Lemonade, see page 202.

Iced Tea, see page 202.

Cousin Ann's Wacky Cake

I used to spend many happy summer days with my cousin Ann Brown. We would make this cake in a jiffy because it was so easy. Now, Ann makes beautifully decorated cakes for weddings and special occasions.

Makes 1 (13 x 9-inch) cake

2 cups sugar	1 tablespoon real vanilla
3 cups all-purpose flour	2 tablespoons vinegar
1/4 cup plus 2 tablespoons	1 3/4 cups butter, softened
cocoa	2 cups cold water
2 teaspoons baking soda	Caramel Frosting
pinch of salt	

Preheat oven to 350 degrees. Combine first 5 ingredients in a large bowl. Add vanilla, vinegar, and butter; beat well. Slowly stir in water; beat well.

Pour batter into an ungreased 13 x 9-inch baking pan. Bake for 35 to 40 minutes or until a wooden pick inserted in center comes out clean. Cool. Spread Caramel Frosting over cake.

Caramel Frosting

Makes enough for 1 (13 x 9-inch) cake

1 1/2 cups firmly packed	1/4 cup plus 2 tablespoons
brown sugar	shortening
1/4 cup plus 2 tablespoons	1/4 teaspoon salt
milk	1/2 teaspoon real vanilla

Combine all ingredients in a medium saucepan; bring to a boil and cook for 1 minute. Remove from heat; beat on medium speed of electric mixer about 10 minutes or until it reaches spreading consistency. Spread frosting on cake immediately.

Moma Norrod's Oatmeal Cake

Moma Norrod, my maternal grandmother, was a wonderful cook. She and Pop Norrod had a country store which fascinated me as a child. I never grew tired of "playing store" with my cousin Jimmy or eating Moma's delicious food.

Serves 20

1 cup oatmeal
1 1/2 cups boiling water
1/2 cup shortening
1 cup brown sugar
1 cup white sugar

2 eggs
1 1/2 cups of flour
1 teaspoon soda
1 teaspoon cinnamon

Preheat oven to 350 degrees. Add oatmeal to water and set aside to cool. Cream shortening, sugar, and eggs; add oatmeal and beat until fluffy. Add dry ingredients sifted together. Bake in greased shallow pan, 13 x 9 x 2 inches, 45 minutes to 1 hour. Add the following topping to cake.

Topping

Makes about 1 cup

1/2 cup butter
1 cup brown sugar
1/2 cup cream

1 cup chopped nuts
1 cup grated coconut
1 teaspoon real vanilla

Combine above and bring to a boil. Spread on cake and brown slightly in oven.

Wanda's Haystack Pie

This is my sister Wanda's creation. Everyone raves about it.

Makes 1 (10-inch) pie

Crust

2 cups chocolate chip cookies,   1/4 cup butter, melted
crumbled

Combine cookies and butter; pat into 10-inch pie pan and bake 4 minutes at 350 degrees.

Filling

1/3 cup sugar	3 egg yolks
pinch salt	4 tablespoons butter
1/3 cup cornstarch	1 teaspoon real vanilla
2 1/2 cups milk	

Combine sugar, salt and cornstarch in saucepan; pour in milk and cook until thick, add egg yolks and butter. Cook 1 minute, add vanilla, pour into pie crust and chill.

Topping

2 sticks butter	1 1/2 cups sugar
2 ounces baking chocolate, melted	4 eggs

Combine butter, chocolate and sugar in large mixing bowl. Beat on high, add eggs, one at a time, beating well after each. Put mixture on top of chilled pie.

Whipped Cream Topping

1 teaspoon hot coffee	2 tablespoons sugar
1/2 teaspoon powdered coffee	1 cup heavy cream, whipped

Add powdered coffee to hot coffee, let cool. Combine whipped cream, sugar and coffee beating until light soft peaks form. Spread on pie.

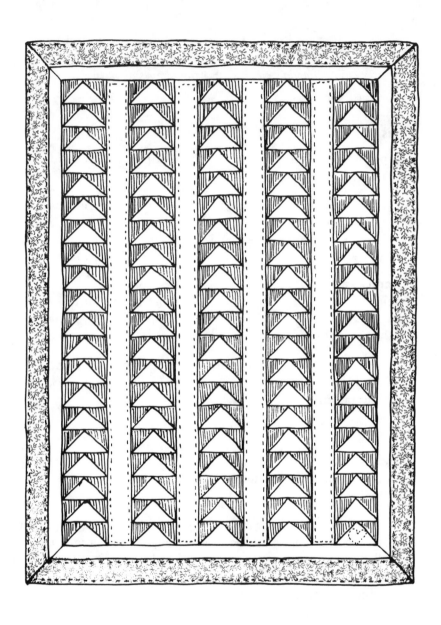

Flying Geese

214

SUMMER BY THE SEA

Here's to the six families at the beach, the Buchanans, the Days, the Dyers, the Gilliams, the McGees and the Worshams, for a week of GREAT FUN, and 25 TEENAGERS plus 3 almost-teenagers. It was fun cooking for such an appreciative audience.

Victor's Ceviche

Joannie's Clam Chowder

Garlicky Good Soft Shell Crabs

Grilled Blackened Wahoo

Corn on the Cob

Homegrown Tomatoes

Rice and Eggplant Medley

Watermelon Fruit Basket

Helen's Pineapple Ice Cream

Easy Ice Cream Cookies

Hubert's Kill Devil Brew

Victor's Ceviche

Victor, of our kitchen staff, being a native of Bolivia, makes a really authentic ceviche. The flavor is exquisitely searing!

2 cups red onions, minced
2 cups celery, minced
1 teaspoon fresh garlic, finely
  chopped
1/2 teaspoon black pepper
1 tablespoon chopped fresh
  parsley
1 tablespoon chopped fresh
  cilantro
1 tablespoon hot banana
  peppers chopped

2 1/2 teaspoons salt
1/2 teaspoon fresh ginger,
  finely chopped
3 pounds firm fleshed white
  fish, fresh
(sole, flounder, grouper or
  scallops)
Fresh squeezed lime juice
Fresh squeezed lemon juice

Cut fish into bite size pieces, add all other ingredients, then cover with the lime and lemon juice. Place in glass pan or bowl. Cover. Marinate overnight. Serve in lettuce lined cocktail or sherbet cups with a wedge of line.

If hotter version desired, add cayenne pepper to taste.

Joannie's Clam Chowder

This is absolutely the creamiest, best tasting chowder there is. All of our kitchen staff makes the greatest soups. I think they try to outdo one another!

1/2 pound butter
8 stalks celery finely chopped
4 carrots finely chopped
2 large yellow onions, finely
  chopped
1 cup flour
4 cups milk
1 3-pound can chopped clams
  in juice or 6 cups chopped
  clams

4 cups heavy cream
1 teaspoon white pepper
1 teaspoon garlic salt
1 1/2 teaspoons thyme
1 teaspoon Old Bay seasoning

Saute the celery, onions, and carrots in the butter until tender. Add the one cup of flour and cook over medium heat approximately 15 minutes. DO NOT BROWN. Add milk, clams and juice, cream, and seasonings. Heat through until slightly thickened. Serve steaming hot with oyster crackers.

Garlicky Good Soft-Shell Crabs

Serves 6

flour	good oil
18 cleaned soft-shell crabs	all the garlic you can stand

To clean crabs: Remove the eyes, sand sac and lower mouth by scissors. Then remove the grey gills which are spongy on either side. Pull down the apron tab and snip it off.

Heat oil in large iron skillet until it sizzles. Saute crabs which have been dusted with flour in the oil with finely chopped garlic a few minutes on each side until done. Remove, keep warm until all crabs are cooked. Salt, pepper, and add a dusting of cayenne pepper if desired. Serve with fresh lemon wedges.

Grilled Blackened Wahoo

This is irresistible!

Follow directions for Blackened Grouper (see page 51), dip wahoo in butter, roll in Victor's Blackening Mixture (see page 51) Instead of cooking in searing skillet, grill over very hot coals on well oiled grill. Takes approximately 15 to 20 minutes depending on thickness of Wahoo steaks.

Other thick fish steaks may be substituted

Rice and Eggplant Medley

Serves 8 to 10

8 tablespoons butter	2 tablespoons Worcestershire
1/2 cup finely chopped onions	salt to taste
1/2 cup finely chopped celery	cayenne pepper to taste
1/2 cup finely chopped green pepper	black pepper to taste
4 cups of finely chopped eggplant	5 cups cooked white rice, hot
1 10 1/2-ounce can beef consomme	1 cup grated Monterey Jack cheese

Preheat oven to 375 degrees. Melt butter, add onions, celery, green pepper and eggplant. Saute until soft. Add rice, consomme and seasonings. Mix well. Put into greased casserole. Top with grated cheese. Bake in preheated oven until cheese melts.

Watermelon Fruit Basket, see page 141.

Helen's Pineapple Ice Cream

Helen Crawford, my neighbor as a child, made the most wonderful ice cream in the summer. I don't know if her secret to success was having her own dairy cow and eggs from her chickens or her ability as a good country cook. She was always willing to let me "pester" her in the kitchen. I just had to have the recipe for this childhood treat.

Makes 2 quarts

2 cups heavy cream	pinch salt
2 cups half and half	1 cup well-drained crushed
3/4 cup sugar	pineapple
1 teaspoon real vanilla	

Combine all ingredients. Freeze in ice cream maker according to manufactures' directions.

Easy Ice Cream Cookies, see page 82.

Hubert's Kill Devil Brew

This is some way to finish a great evening.

Good strong hot coffee	Freshly grated nutmeg
Wild Turkey Liqueur	
Stiffly Whipped Cream,	
sweetened	

Place a jigger of the liqueur in coffee mug, fill with coffee. Top with sweetened whipped cream. Dust with grated nutmeg.

Ocean Waves

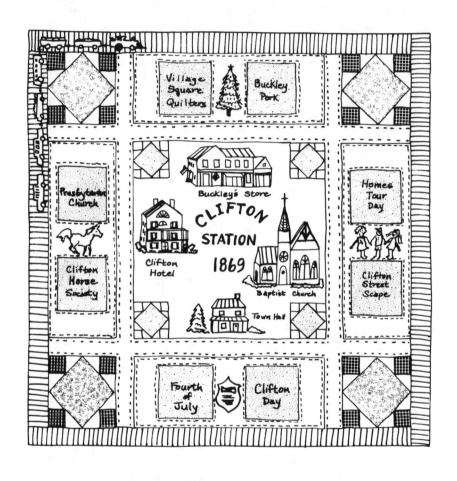

Town of Clifton Quilt

220

CLIFTON DAY

Hot Spiced Cider
Clifton Day Brunswick Stew
Sweet and Sour Coleslaw
Bite-size Cornmeal Muffins
Autumn Apple Crisp

Hot Spiced Cider

With the first autumn chill, nothing is better than a mug of hot cider. Try to buy freshly pressed or natural style cider.

Serves 6-8

1 teaspoon whole allspice	2 quarts apple cider
12 whole cloves	Freshly grated nutmeg
2 2-inch cinnamon sticks	1 thinly sliced lemon
1/2 cup brown sugar	

Tie allspice, cinnamon, and cloves in a cheesecloth bag. In stainless steel or enameled saucepan combine brown sugar and cider. Heat to boiling, add spice bag and reduce to simmer for 10 minutes.

Serve hot with dash of nutmeg on each and one thin lemon slice.

Clifton Day Brunswick Stew

On Clifton Day, we see the lines forming earlier and longer as people anticipate the stew being served each year.

Makes 1 gallon

Day 1

1 five-to-six pound stewing hen	4 quarts water
1 stalk of celery	1 fresh hot red pepper, 3 to 5
1 large carrot	inches long
1 large yellow onion	3 whole bay leaves
1 handful fresh parsley	1/4 cup salt
1 10-ounce can tomato puree	

Put all the above ingredients in a large stockpot, bring to a boil and simmer slowly, covered, for about four hours. Let cool and strain, saving strained liquid. Pull chicken meat off bones and pull into bite size pieces. Return to strained broth and refrigerate.

Day Two

6 yellow onions, finely chopped	2 cups celery, finely sliced
2 green peppers, finely chopped	1 lemon, peeled into one continuous strip and juiced approximately two tablespoons
2 turnips, finely chopped	1 tablespoon fresh thyme, or
1 28-ounce can tomatoes, in juice, diced	1 1/2 teaspoons dried thyme
2 cups lima beans, fresh or frozen	2 tablespoons Worcestershire
2 cups yellow corn, fresh or frozen	2 tablespoons sugar
2 cups okra, sliced, fresh or frozen	1 tablespoon hot pepper sauce (or to taste)
2 cups cabbage, finely sliced	salt to taste
	pepper to taste, freshly ground, black

Put Day One's mixture on top of stove, add all of day two's ingredients and simmer two hours (or until thickened). Taste for seasoning and add any additional seasonings.

Please watch pot, do not let stick.

If reheating mixture, heat in oven or microwave to insure against scorching. We always serve in our Heart in Hand pottery mugs with a sprinkling of chopped green onions. This is a wonderful cold weather meal-in-itself dish!

Sweet and Sour Coleslaw

This coleslaw is great for a crowd. It is easy to fix as well as a good keeper.
Serves 12-16

5-6 pounds cabbage, shredded
2 medium carrots, shredded
2 green peppers, shredded
2 large Vidalia or red onions,
  chopped
1 cup apple-cider vinegar

1 1/2 cups peanut or corn oil
1 1/2 teaspoons salt
1 teaspoon celery seeds
1 teaspoon mustard seeds
1/2 to 1 cup sugar

Combine the vegetables in a large bowl. Put oil, vinegar, mustard seeds, celery seeds, and sugar in a saucepan and bring to a boil. Pour over cabbage mixture and toss. Chill mixture, stirring from time to time.

Bite Size Cornmeal Muffins

Makes 36-48

1 1/2 cup self-rising cornmeal
1 cup self-rising flour
1/3 cup sugar

1 1/2 cups milk
3/4 cup oil, corn or vegetable
2 eggs, beaten

Preheat the oven to 500 degrees. Combine dry ingredients in bowl, make well in center, combine liquid ingredients with beaten eggs, add to dry and beat until smooth. Spoon into well greased miniature muffin tins, 2/3 full. Bake 8 to 10 minutes.

Use a white self-rising cornmeal mix, preferably stone-ground.

Autumn Apple Crisp

The fall crop of crisp, juicy Virginia apples beckons us to make this!
Serves 6

Apple mixture:

4 cups apples, sliced, peeled,
   1/4 inch thick
1/2 cup orange juice
3/4 cup sugar

1/2 teaspoon cinnamon
1/2 teaspoon freshly grated
   nutmeg

Topping mixture:

1/2 cup butter
1 cup dry oats
1/2 cup flour

1/2 cup brown sugar, firmly
   packed
1/2 cup chopped pecans

Preheat the oven to 350 degrees. Spray 2-quart casserole with vegetable spray. Combine apple mixture. Put into dish. Melt butter in microwave or on top of stove. Add remaining ingredients. Crumble on top of apple mixture. Bake 30 to 45 minutes until apples are done (DO NOT OVERBAKE). Serve warm with ice cream or whipped cream.

Sampler

THE SEXY SEVEN'S LUNCHEON

Six of my very good friends and I celebrate Christmas and birthdays on the same day. It is a day full of good food and drink, lots of presents, and a renewing of our friendships. We range in age from mid-thirties to the mid-sixties and have many similar yet varied interests. This is a fun luncheon for your best of friends. Put on party hats, set the table extra special and have a ball!

Donna Nickum's Cucumber Punch

Betty Boyd's Crabmeat Spread

Diane Smith's Shrimp Diane

Bev Lozito's Tangy Tarragon Dressing

Bette Faries' Braided Bread and Raisin Bread

Shelva Rota's Sinfully Rich Cheesecake

Donna Nickum's Cucumber Punch

This is delicious but can sneak up on you...

Makes 1 gallon

1/4 pound powdered sugar
2 oz. brandy
4 oz. curacao

2 oz. Maraschino liqueur
2 quarts mineral water
2 quarts Champagne

Mix these in a punch bowl that has been set in a bank of ice. Decorate with fresh fruits and add cucumber slices that have been grooved for a unique flare.

Betty Boyd's Crabmeat Spread

This is so creamy and easy to make.

Serves 6

1 (8-ounce) cream cheese, softened
1 tablespoon milk
6 1/2 ounce fresh flaked crabmeat
2 tablespoons finely chopped onions

1/2 teaspoon horseradish, cream style
1/4 teaspoon salt
dash pepper
1/3 cup sliced almonds, toasted

Preheat oven to 375 degrees. Combine cream cheese with milk; add crabmeat, onions, horseradish, salt, and pepper. Blend well and put in a small ovenproof dish. Sprinkle almonds on top. Bake, uncovered, for 15 minutes. Serve with crackers.

Can be made ahead and freezes very well.

Diane Smith's Shrimp Diane

Diane is a very good cook. This is her creation.

Serves 8

3 pounds raw deveined shrimp
12 fresh mushrooms, diced
4 green onions, chopped fine
1/2 cup chopped celery
4 slices prosciutto ham sliced
in strips
2 teaspoons granulated
chicken bouillon

4 ounces butter
1 pint heavy cream (more if
needed)
1/2 cup sherry
1 teaspoon paprika
ground white pepper to taste

Melt butter in saucepan, add green onion, celery, mushrooms, ham and chicken bouillon. Saute at least five minutes over high heat. Add shrimp and cook five more minutes. Lower heat. Combine cream, sherry, paprika, pepper and add to saucepan. Cook for five more minutes. Serve over rice.

Bev Lozito's Tangy Tarragon Dressing

This is sophisticated in taste.

Makes about 1 1/3 cups

1 cup salad oil
grated peel of 1 fresh lemon
juice of 2 fresh lemons
2 tablespoons honey

1 tablespoon dijon mustard
1/2 teaspoon onion salt
1/2 teaspoon (or to taste) dried
tarragon - crushed

In a jar with lid, combine all dressing ingredients. Chill. Shake well before serving.

Serve with a mixed green salad.

Use a good variety of lettuces and include some watercress and fresh spinach for flavor.

Bette Faries' Braided Bread and Raisin Bread

Bette is a true breadmaker. She always gives us gorgeous loaves to use for the holidays.

6 3/4 to 7 cups all-purpose
   flour
2 packages active dry yeast
2 cups milk
4 tablespoons butter or
   margarine

1/4 cup granulated sugar
1 tablespoon salt
3 eggs
1 cup raisins

Icing

1/2 cup powdered sugar   milk

In large mixer bowl, combine 3 cups of the flour and the yeast. In saucepan, heat the two cups milk, the butter or margarine, granulated sugar and salt just till warm (115 to 120 degrees), stirring constantly till butter almost melts. Add to dry ingredients in mixer bowl; add eggs. Beat at low speed of electric mixer for 1/2 minute, scraping sides of bowl constantly. Beat 3 minutes at high speed. By hand, stir in enough of the remaining flour to make a moderately stiff dough. Turn out onto floured surface. Knead till smooth and elastic, 5 to 8 minutes. Place in greased bowl, turn once to grease surface. Cover; let rise till double, about 1 hour. Divide dough in 3 parts. Knead raisins into 1 part; cover and let rest 10 minutes. Divide remaining two parts in 3 portions each. Cover; let rest 10 minutes. Shape raisin dough in round loaf. Place on greased baking sheet; cover. On floured surface, roll the six smaller pieces in ropes 15 inches long. On greased baking sheet, line up three of the ropes. Braid loosely, beginning in the middle and working toward the ends. Pinch ends and turn under. Repeat with remaining three ropes. Cover; let all loaves rise till double, about 1 hour. Bake braids and raisin loaf in 375-degree oven for 20 to 25 minutes. Makes 2 braids and 1 raisin loaf.

Shelva Rota's Sinfully Rich Cheesecake

Very expensive, very fattening, but very, very delicious!

4 8-ounce packages of cream
cheese, softened
3 eggs, separated
1/2 pint whipping cream
3/4 cup sugar
3/4 cup Liqueur Galliano
1 6-ounce package of
chocolate chips

1 lb. shelled pecans, chopped
1/8 cup water
1 tablespoon sugar
2 envelopes unflavored gelatin
1/4 cup water

Beat softened cheese until quite fluffy. Add egg yolks and 1/2 cup sugar, combine thoroughly. Soften gelatin in 1/4 cup cold water, dissolve over very low heat, cool until syrupy, then mix into the cheese mixture and beat well. Add Galliano to cheese mixture and mix well. Beat egg whites stiff, adding 1/4 cup sugar, then fold into cheese mixture. Whip cream stiff, then fold into cheese mixture.

Meanwhile melt chocolate over very low heat, adding 1/8 cup water and 1 tablespoon sugar. Combine with chopped pecans, let cool slightly for easy handling. Line inside of a well-buttered springform pan with 3/4 of the pecan/chocolate mixture. Pour cheese into pan and sprinkle with 1/4 reserved mixture over the top. Refrigerate overnight or freeze 3 to 4 hours before serving.

INDEX

A

Index

Index

Index

Index

Index

Index

Index

Cooking with Heart in Hand
P.O. Box 170, 7145 Main St.
Clifton, Virginia 22024

Please send _____ copies of COOKING WITH HEART IN HAND.
Enclosed you will find $14.95 per book, plus $2.95 postage and
handling per book. Virginia residents add 4½% sales tax. (Please
make checks payable to Heart in Hand, Inc.)

Name _____

Address _____

City _____ State _____ Zip _____

- -

Cooking with Heart in Hand
P.O. Box 170, 7145 Main St.
Clifton, Virginia 22024

Please send _____ copies of COOKING WITH HEART IN HAND.
Enclosed you will find $14.95 per book, plus $2.95 postage and
handling per book. Virginia residents add 4½% sales tax. (Please
make checks payable to Heart in Hand, Inc.)

Name _____

Address _____

City _____ State _____ Zip _____

- -

Cooking with Heart in Hand
P.O. Box 170, 7145 Main St.
Clifton, Virginia 22024

Please send _____ copies of COOKING WITH HEART IN HAND.
Enclosed you will find $14.95 per book, plus $2.95 postage and
handling per book. Virginia residents add 4½% sales tax. (Please
make checks payable to Heart in Hand, Inc.)

Name _____

Address _____

City _____ State _____ Zip _____

Reorder Additional Copies